Math

GRADES 2–3

Energize your math lessons and strengthen students' math skills with this timesaving collection of reproducible activities. The activities were selected from issues of Grades 2–3 *Teacher's Helper®* magazine published between 1994 and 1999.

THE BEST OF TEACHER'S HELPER® Magazine

Editor:
Njeri Jones Legrand

Art Coordinator:
Teresa R. Davidson

Cover Designer:
Jennifer L. Tipton

Cover Artist:
Nick Greenwood

www.themailbox.com

©2000 by THE EDUCATION CENTER, INC.
All rights reserved.
ISBN# 1-56234-356-4

Manufactured in the United States
10 9 8 7 6 5 4 3 2

Table of Contents

Cool Sailing

Captain Cone and his crew are searching for ice-cream treasure.
In each ☐ , copy the number in the 🍦 .
Add.

A. ☐
  $+ 5$

  2
  $+$ ☐

  ☐
  $+ 8$

  6
  $+$ ☐

  ☐
  $+ 1$

  9
  $+$ ☐

B. 8
  $+$ ☐

  0
  $+$ ☐

  ☐
  $+ 7$

  ☐
  $+ 4$

  ☐
☐
  $+$

  3
  $+$ ☐

C. ☐
  $+ 2$

  5
  $+$ ☐

  ☐
  $+ 9$

  ☐
  $+ 8$

  1
  $+$ ☐

  ☐
  $+ 6$

D. 8
  $+$ ☐

  ☐
  $+ 3$

  ☐
  $+ 2$

  7
  $+$ ☐

  ☐
  $+ 2$

  4
  $+$ ☐

E. ☐ $+ 9$ = _____   ☐ $+ 3$ = _____

  $7 +$ ☐ = _____   ☐ $+$ ☐ = _____

  ☐ $+ 4$ = _____ $0 +$ ☐ = _____

Bonus Box: Draw a scoop of ice cream around each sum. If the sum is even, use a red crayon.
If the sum is odd, use a brown crayon. Then complete the treasure tally.

Treasure Tally: strawberry scoops = _____   chocolate scoops = _____

How To Use This Addition Unit
Pages 3–10

Yo, ho, ho! Sweeten your students' appetites for addition with these cool and creamy reproducibles. It's a booty of math practice that's simply delicious!

How To Use Page 3

1. Make a copy of page 3. Program the 🍦 with a desired addend; then duplicate student copies plus one. (Use the extra copy to make an answer key.)
2. Distribute the student copies and have each child complete the activity as directed.

Background For The Teacher
Ice Cream

Ice cream—an irresistible dessert to many—has been around for a long time. No one knows for sure when ice cream was first made; however, it is believed that British colonists brought recipes for ice cream to America in the early 1700s. The dessert soon became a popular luxury food. Almost all ice cream was made in the home until 1851, when a Baltimore milk dealer established the first ice-cream plant. The arrival of soda fountains—along with new ways of serving ice cream in sodas, sundaes, cones, and ice-cream sandwiches—propelled the cool and creamy dessert to become a national favorite in the early 1900s.

Ice cream is served in many parts of the world. However, Americans eat more of it than any other nation's people—about 15 quarts per person per year! The milk products in ice cream make it rich in calcium, phosphorus, protein, and vitamin A. The fats and carbohydrates it contains make it high in calories.

Book Corner

Ice Cream
From Cow To Ice Cream • Written & Photographed by Bertram T. Knight • Childrens Press®, Inc.; 1997

Let's Find Out About Ice Cream • Written by Mary Ebeltoft Reid & Photographed by John Williams • Scholastic Inc., 1997

Ben & Jerry: Ice Cream For Everyone! • Written by Keith Elliot Greenberg & Illustrated by Dave Kilmer • A Blackbirch Press Book, 1994

Name _____

Tasty Treasure

In each treasure chest:

Solve each fact.

Cross out the matching sum on the lid.

Write the extra sum in the box.

Then write an addition fact that equals
the sum.

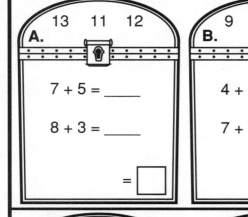

A. 13 11 12

$7 + 5 =$ _____

$8 + 3 =$ _____

$=$ ☐

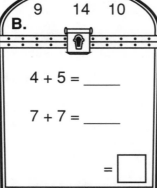

B. 9 14 10

$4 + 5 =$ _____

$7 + 7 =$ _____

$=$ ☐

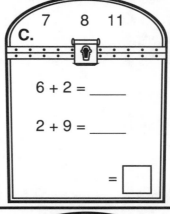

C. 7 8 11

$6 + 2 =$ _____

$2 + 9 =$ _____

$=$ ☐

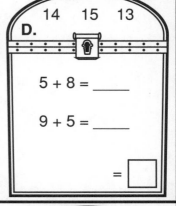

D. 14 15 13

$5 + 8 =$ _____

$9 + 5 =$ _____

$=$ ☐

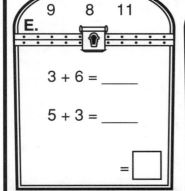

E. 9 8 11

$3 + 6 =$ _____

$5 + 3 =$ _____

$=$ ☐

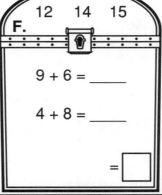

F. 12 14 15

$9 + 6 =$ _____

$4 + 8 =$ _____

$=$ ☐

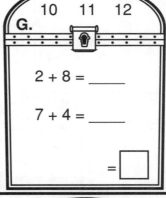

G. 10 11 12

$2 + 8 =$ _____

$7 + 4 =$ _____

$=$ ☐

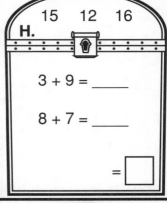

H. 15 12 16

$3 + 9 =$ _____

$8 + 7 =$ _____

$=$ ☐

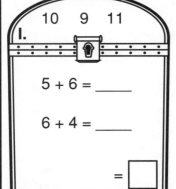

I. 10 9 11

$5 + 6 =$ _____

$6 + 4 =$ _____

$=$ ☐

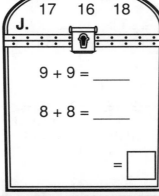

J. 17 16 18

$9 + 9 =$ _____

$8 + 8 =$ _____

$=$ ☐

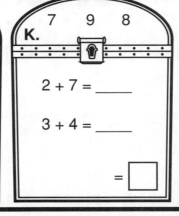

K. 7 9 8

$2 + 7 =$ _____

$3 + 4 =$ _____

$=$ ☐

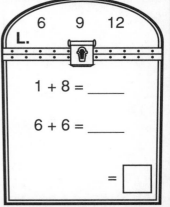

L. 6 9 12

$1 + 8 =$ _____

$6 + 6 =$ _____

$=$ ☐

Bonus Box: On the back of this paper, draw two treasure chests. On one treasure chest, write two different
sums on the lid. Then, on the chest, write an addition fact that equals each sum. On the other chest, draw and
color a treasure you would like to find!

Answer Key

*(The student-created problem in each chest will vary,
but should equal the provided sum.)*

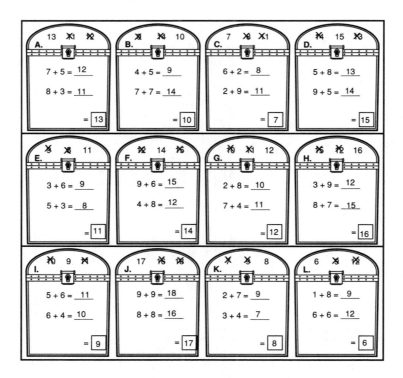

Name _____

Cones For The Crew

Find out the cost of each pirate's ice-cream cone.
Use the Pirate Prices.
Show your work.

1. Daring Dan: 1 scoop peach 1 scoop strawberry 1 spoonful sprinkles	**2. Jolly Julie:** 1 scoop nutty surprise 1 scoop chocolate 2 spoonfuls sprinkles	**3. Crazy Cal:** 1 scoop cherry 1 scoop mint 3 spoonfuls sprinkles	**4. Sweet-Tooth Sue:** 1 scoop peppermint 1 scoop licorice 1 spoonful sprinkles
5. Cannonball Kurt: 1 scoop walnut 1 scoop lemon 2 spoonfuls sprinkles	**6. Wise Willy:** 1 scoop vanilla 1 scoop butternut 1 spoonful sprinkles	**7. Slim Jim:** 1 scoop fudge 1 scoop hazelnut 1 scoop orange	**8. Tough Teresa:** 1 scoop pineapple 1 scoop nutty crunch 2 spoonfuls sprinkles

PIRATE PRICES

ice cream per scoop		sprinkles per spoonful	
fruit flavor .... 20¢		1 .... 10¢	
nut flavor .... 25¢		2 .... 12¢	
all other flavors .... 30¢		3 .... 15¢	

Bonus Box: Color each pirate's ice-cream cone. If you like, color the cones so they match the ice-cream orders above.

Suggestion For Reprogramming Page 7

To increase the difficulty of page 7, make a copy of the page. White-out the money amounts in "Pirate Prices" and replace them with larger amounts and/or amounts that require students to regroup. Then duplicate the activity and create a corresponding answer key.

Answer Key

1. Daring Dan
   20¢
   20¢
   10¢
   50¢

2. Jolly Julie
   25¢
   30¢
   12¢
   67¢

3. Crazy Cal
   20¢
   30¢
   15¢
   65¢

4. Sweet-Tooth Sue
   30¢
   30¢
   10¢
   70¢

5. Cannonball Kurt
   25¢
   20¢
   12¢
   57¢

6. Wise Willy
   30¢
   25¢
   10¢
   65¢

7. Slim Jim
   30¢
   25¢
   20¢
   75¢

8. Tough Teresa
   20¢
   25¢
   12¢
   57¢

A Cone-Eating Contest

Which pirate wins the contest?
Solve each problem below. Cut on the dotted lines.

Ernie

Ozzie

Now do this!

If a sum is **even**, glue the cone beside Ernie.

If a sum is **odd**, glue the cone beside Ozzie.

Then:
Put a drop of glue on each ●.
Glue each ribbon in place.

1st   2nd

41
+ 31

60
+ 23

52
+ 22

31
+ 27

74
+ 14

86
+ 13

32
+ 33

27
+ 42

63
+ 15

54
+ 32

14
+ 25

Suggestions For Reprogramming Page 9

For three-digit addition practice without regrouping, make a copy of the page. Add a hundreds digit to each number—taking care to not create a need for regrouping. Then duplicate the activity and create a corresponding answer key.

For two-digit addition practice with regrouping, make a copy of the page. White-out one digit per problem. Replace each missing digit with one that creates a need to regroup. Take care to maintain six even-numbered answers and five odd-numbered answers (or vice versa). Then duplicate the activity and create a corresponding answer key.

For three-digit addition practice with regrouping, make a copy of the page. Add a hundreds digit to each number—creating a few regrouping opportunities. For each remaining problem that does not require regrouping, white-out one digit and replace it with a digit that creates a need to regroup. Take care to maintain six even-numbered answers and five odd-numbered answers (or vice versa). Then duplicate the activity and create a corresponding answer key.

Answer Key

(The order of cones in each row will vary.)

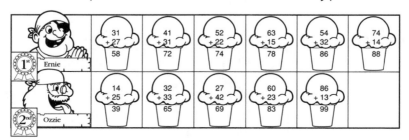

Name_____

"Unbe-leaf-able" Fun

In each , copy the number on the tree.
Add.

A.   4 +___   + 9   0 +___   + 3

B.   5 +___   + 8   6 +___   + 2

C.   1 +___   + 7   8 +___   + 9

D.   9 +___   + 4   7 +___   + 6

E.   + 0 = _____   + = _____

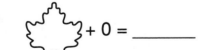 5 + = _____    7 +  = _____

Bonus Box: On the back of this sheet, write about two times you used addition in real life.

How To Use This Fall Foliage Math Unit
Pages 11–18

Use this fall-related collection of reproducible activities to get your youngsters' computation skills off to a "tree-mendous" start! These math activities can easily be incorporated into a fall unit, or they can be used collectively or independently at any time.

How To Use Page 11

1. Make a copy of page 11. Program the hole in the tree with a desired addend; then duplicate a class supply of copies plus one extra copy. (Use the extra copy to make an answer key.)
2. Distribute the student copies and have each child complete the activity as directed.

Extension Activity

Get your youngsters falling for math activities that are sure to reinforce a variety of skills! Duplicate a class supply of the student management sheet on page 14. Then make each student a folder by folding a 12" x 18" sheet of green construction paper in half. Place at least three sheets of writing paper inside each folder. Glue a copy of the student management sheet to the front of each folder. Next provide each youngster with a medium-sized paper bag; then take your class on a leaf-gathering expedition. When each student returns with his leaf-filled bag, distribute the folders. Have each student personalize his folder. During free time, have each youngster use his leaves to complete the activities on his student management sheet. Then have him store his completed work in the folder. These math "leaf-ercises" are sure to provide a pile of fun-filled math practice!

Background For The Teacher
Fall Leaves

As any dendrologist (person who studies trees) will tell you, the study of trees and their autumn leaves is a colorful one! Deciduous, or broadleaf, trees provide us with a brilliant display every autumn before they shed their leaves for the winter.

Fall leaf colors include red, yellow, orange, and brown. The color depends on the species of tree, the weather, and the soil. Red is produced by warm days and cool nights that turn leftover food in the leaf into red pigment. Leaves turn orange or yellow when the green chlorophyll, which hides other colors present in the leaf, is destroyed by the cold.

The black tupelo and the flowering dogwood usually turn bright scarlet. For brilliant yellows, look for birches, aspens, and alders. Leaves on the American beech usually turn brown, with other trees providing a mix of these colors. On a single tree, like a sugar maple, you may see leaves of several colors all at the same time. Other trees, like the sweet gum, may turn different colors at different times. It's a breathtaking show, seen at its best in the northeast United States.

Name

Fresh Fall Leaves

Add the numbers on the leaves of each tree.
Write and solve the problem on each tree trunk.

a.

b.

c.

d.

e.

f.

g.

h.

i.

j.

Bonus Box: Look at the number on each leaf. If the number is odd, color the leaf orange. If the number is even, color the leaf brown.

Answer Key

(Order of addends in each problem may vary.)

a.	b.	c.	d.	e.
6	8	5	4	5
5	4	6	3	2
+ 4	+ 3	+ 6	+ 4	+ 5
15	15	17	11	12

f.	g.	h.	i.	j.
3	5	7	1	2
4	9	2	8	3
+ 1	+ 4	+ 7	+ 4	+ 9
8	18	16	13	14

Student Management Sheet

Use with the extension activity on page 12.

Name _____ Student Management Sheet

Fabulous Fall Foliage

Color each leaf when you have completed the activity.

1. Use your leaves to create a pattern. Draw the pattern.

2. Make a list of five addition problems that equal the sum of your leaves.

3. Sort your leaves by color. Make a graph to show the information.

4. Choose five leaves. Describe the color, shape, and size of each one.

5. Measure and write the length of each leaf.

6. Use your leaves to write three word problems.

Name_____

Turning Over A New Leaf

Solve each problem.
Color the leaf with the matching answer.

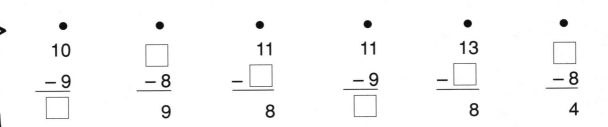

12	16	☐	15	18	☐
− ☐	− 8	− 6	− 9	− ☐	− 5
5	☐	4	☐	9	6

10	☐	11	11	13	☐
− 9	− 8	− ☐	− 9	− ☐	− 8
☐	9	8	☐	8	4

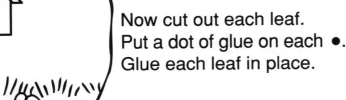

Now cut out each leaf.
Put a dot of glue on each ●.
Glue each leaf in place.

Bonus Box: On a separate sheet of paper, write a word problem that can be solved by using subtraction. Be sure to answer the problem too!

©The Education Center, Inc. • *The Best of* Teacher's Helper® *Math* • TEC3212

17   10   2   7   1   6

12   8   5   11   9   3

15

Materials Needed For Each Student

— crayons

— scissors

— glue

How To Use Page 15

This activity is designed to reinforce basic subtraction skills. Distribute the materials listed below. Then have students follow the directions on the sheet to complete the activity.

Completed Sample

Answer Key

12 $-\boxed{7}$ 5	16 -8 $\boxed{8}$	$\boxed{10}$ -6 4	15 -9 $\boxed{6}$	18 $-\boxed{9}$ 9	$\boxed{11}$ -5 6
10 -9 $\boxed{1}$	$\boxed{17}$ -8 9	11 $-\boxed{3}$ 8	11 -9 $\boxed{2}$	13 $-\boxed{5}$ 8	$\boxed{12}$ -8 4

Bonus Box Answer: Answers will vary.

Name_____

Birds Of A Feather

Add or subtract.

6
+ 4

5
+ 8

8
+ 7

10
− 6

15
− 7

3
+ 9

9
+ 3

4
+ 6

13
− 5

12
− 9

15
− 8

8
+ 5

10
− 4

7
+ 8

13
− 8

12
− 3

3 9 12
red

4 6 10
orange

7 8 15
yellow

5 8 13
brown

Now try this!
Look at the birds'
numbers on each
branch.
Use the color code
to color each leaf in
the fact family.

Bonus Box: On the back of this sheet, write the four facts in the fact family for 5, 6, and 11.

©The Education Center, Inc. • *The Best of* Teacher's Helper® *Math* • TEC3212

17

How To Use Page 17

This activity is designed to give students practice with fact families. Before getting started, give students a quick review of fact families.

Answer Key

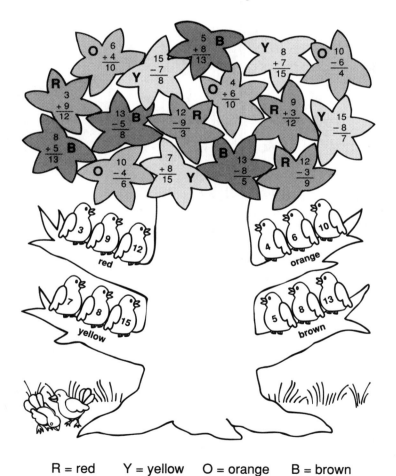

R = red   Y = yellow   O = orange   B = brown

Bonus Box Answer: *(Order of students' answers will vary.)*

5 + 6 = 11	6 + 5 = 11	11 - 5 = 6	11 - 6 = 5

Name_____

Riding To The Top!

Solve the problems.
Show your work.

Why did the "unhoppy" bunny decide to go snow skiing?

LOST HAT PASS

16 + 15 = E	26 + 27 = H
17 + 24 = E	49 + 23 = N	57 + 37 = S
26 + 19 = L	36 + 54 = A	19 + 45 = B

38 + 23 = E	55 + 15 = I	37 + 38 = E	37 + 45 = D	49 + 19 = U	45 + 46 = T
68 + 15 = A	48 + 38 = E	38 + 19 = D	17 + 59 = F	57 + 23 = C	29 + 48 = E

To solve the riddle, match the letters to the numbered lines below.

__ __ __ __ __ __ __   __ __
64 41 80 83 68 94 86   53 75

__ __ __ __ __ __   __   __ __ __ __ **!**
72 61 31 57 77 82   90   45 70 76 91

Bonus Box: How else could you get to the top of a mountain? Write the different ways on the back of this sheet.

Lift-Ticket Awards

Here's a fun way to give your youngsters a lift! Using the patterns below, duplicate, cut out, and hole-punch a supply of construction-paper awards. You will also need a supply of one-foot yarn lengths. To present an award, program it (sign and date the back of the award if desired); then thread and loop a yarn length through the hole as shown. The award can be tied to a child's clothing (such as a belt loop or buttonhole) or tied around a child's wrist. Too cool!

Erin
knows all of the
right moves
when it comes to
doing
her math
homework.

Answer Key

LOST HAT PASS

		16 +15 31 = E	26 +27 53 = H
	17 +24 41 = E	49 +23 72 = N	57 +37 94 = S
	26 +19 45 = L	36 +54 90 = A	19 +45 64 = B

38 +23 61 = E	55 +15 70 = I	37 +38 75 = E	37 +45 82 = D	49 +19 68 = U	45 +46 91 = T
68 +15 83 = A	48 +38 86 = E	38 +19 57 = D	17 +59 76 = F	57 +23 80 = C	29 +48 77 = E

B E C A U S E   H E
64 41 80 83 68 94 86   53 75

N E E D E D   A   L I F T !
72 61 31 57 77 82   90   45 70 76 91

Bonus Box: How else could you get to the top of a mountain? Write the different ways on the back of this sheet.

knows all of the
right moves
when it comes to

knows all of the
right moves
when it comes to

Name _____

Snow Skiing
Two-digit addition with
and without regrouping

Cool Caps

Solve the problems.
Show your work.

```
 63        29        52        45
+19       +31       +36       +39
```

CAP SALE!

```
 45        56        73        25
+25       +18       +22       +14
```

```
 57        47        19        67
+27       +41       +55       +28
```

CAP SALE!

```
 16        31
+23       +39
```

```
 28        20
+54       +40
```

For each cap find another cap with the same answer.
Color the matching caps exactly the same.
You may use as many different colors as you like.

Bonus Box: Pretend you have just been given a magic ski cap that will grant
you one wish. Draw and color a picture of the ski cap on the back of this
sheet. Write your wish; then write who you would give the cap to next and why.

21

Extension Activity

For added reinforcement of math word problems or other desired math skills, have students make and keep math journals. Each student will need two construction-paper copies of the pattern below, several half-sheets of blank paper, scissors, crayons or markers, and access to a stapler. To make a journal, cut out the two patterns. Using one pattern as a template, trace and cut out a desired number of journal pages from the blank paper. To create a reversible journal (a journal that can be used from front to back and back to front), personalize and decorate both journal covers, then align and staple the blank journal pages between the embellished covers.

Each day have students complete a math task in their journals. To reinforce word problems, ask students to calculate the answer to a provided word problem or challenge students to create and solve original word problems. Later ask a student volunteer to provide the solution to the daily math challenge or invite students to share their original problems and corresponding solutions for their classmates' approval.

Pattern
Use with the extension activity on this page.

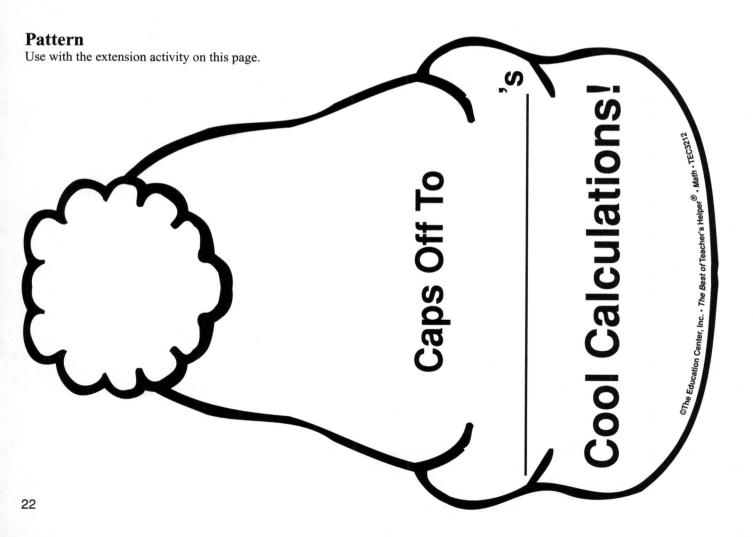

Name _____

Zigging And Zagging

Show your stuff!
Use the two numbers on each snowy bump to write a subtraction problem.

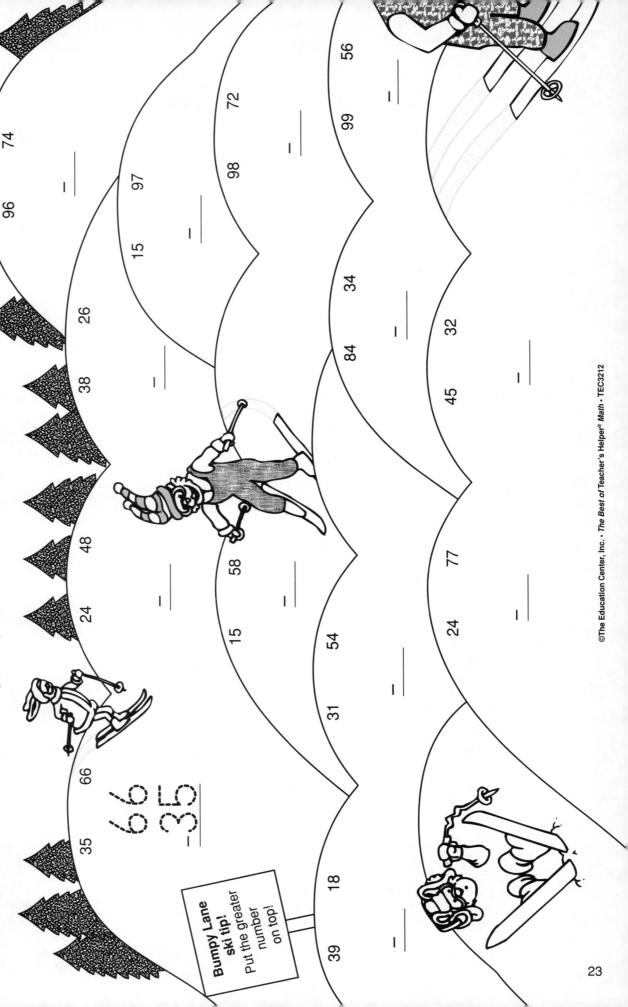

96 74
__

97
15 __

98 72
__

99 56
__ __

26
38 __

34
84 __

32
45 __

48
24 __

58
15 __

54
31 __

77
24 __ __

18

39 __

$$\begin{array}{r} 66 \\ -35 \\ \hline \end{array}$$

**Bumpy Lane
ski tip!**
Put the greater
number
on top!

35
66

23

Answer Key

Bumpy Lane ski tip! Put the greater number on top!

35   66

$$\begin{array}{r} 66 \\ -35 \\ \hline \mathbf{31} \end{array}$$

24   48

$$\begin{array}{r} 48 \\ -24 \\ \hline 24 \end{array}$$

38   26

$$\begin{array}{r} 38 \\ -26 \\ \hline 12 \end{array}$$

96   74

$$\begin{array}{r} 96 \\ -74 \\ \hline 22 \end{array}$$

15   58

$$\begin{array}{r} 58 \\ -15 \\ \hline 43 \end{array}$$

15   97

$$\begin{array}{r} 97 \\ -15 \\ \hline 82 \end{array}$$

98   72

$$\begin{array}{r} 98 \\ -72 \\ \hline 26 \end{array}$$

39   18

$$\begin{array}{r} 39 \\ -18 \\ \hline 21 \end{array}$$

31   54

$$\begin{array}{r} 54 \\ -31 \\ \hline 23 \end{array}$$

84   34

$$\begin{array}{r} 84 \\ -34 \\ \hline 50 \end{array}$$

99   56

$$\begin{array}{r} 99 \\ -56 \\ \hline 43 \end{array}$$

24   77

$$\begin{array}{r} 77 \\ -24 \\ \hline 53 \end{array}$$

45   32

$$\begin{array}{r} 45 \\ -32 \\ \hline 13 \end{array}$$

Name

A One-Of-A-Kind Skier

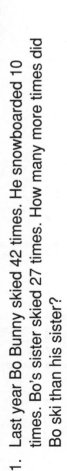

Carefully read each problem.
Circle the sentence that tells what you need to find out.
Cross out any information you don't need.
Solve the problem in the matching box below.

1. Last year Bo Bunny skied 42 times. He snowboarded 10 times. Bo's sister skied 27 times. How many more times did Bo ski than his sister?

2. Next month Bo is planning a ski trip to Hare Mountain. The trip costs $75. Bo has saved $29. How many more dollars does Bo need?

3. During the winter Bo Bunny eats a lot of carrots. His mom gave him 94 carrots. Bo has eaten 27 carrots and 29 turnips. How many carrots are left?

4. Bo collects autographs from famous athletes. He has autographs from 36 skiers and 63 hockey players. Bo hopes to have 50 skiers' autographs by February. How many more skiers' autographs does he need?

5. To stay in shape, Bo Bunny swims laps. This week he swam 35 laps on Monday, 25 laps on Wednesday, and 16 laps on Friday. How many more laps did he swim on Monday than on Friday?

6. Bo waxes his skis so he can ski fast! He had 66 cans of ski wax. He used 49 cans of wax and 26 waxing cloths. How many cans of wax are left?

7. Last week the chairlift had 84 red chairs and 22 green chairs. This morning Bo saw a worker remove 16 red chairs. How many red chairs are left?

8. Bo Bunny had 56 different ski caps. He gave 17 of the ski caps to the bunnies in the beginning ski class. How many ski caps does he have left?

9. Bo began the day with 83¢. About midmorning he paid 57¢ for a mug of hot carrot juice. His skiing buddy bought a turnip roll for 55¢. How much money does Bo have left?

10. Hans Hare holds the record for the longest ski jump with a jump of 93 feet. Bo Bunny jumped 70 feet on Thursday. On Friday he jumped 77 feet. To tie Hans's record, how many more feet does Bo need to jump?

1.	2.	3.	4.	5.
6.	7.	8.	9.	10.

Answer Key

1. Last year Bo Bunny skied 42 times. ~~He snowboarded 10 times.~~ Bo's sister skied 27 times. (How many more times did Bo ski than his sister?)

2. Next month Bo is planning a ski trip to Hare Mountain. The trip costs $75. Bo has saved $29. (How many more dollars does Bo need?)

3. During the winter Bo Bunny eats a lot of carrots. His mom gave him 94 carrots. Bo has eaten 27 carrots ~~and 20 turnips.~~ (How many carrots are left?)

4. Bo collects autographs from famous athletes. He has autographs from 36 skiers ~~and 63 hockey players.~~ Bo hopes to have 50 skiers' autographs by February. (How many more skiers' autographs does he need?)

5. To stay in shape, Bo Bunny swims laps. This week he swam 35 laps on Monday, ~~25 laps on Wednesday,~~ and 16 laps on Friday. (How many more laps did he swim on Monday than on Friday?)

6. Bo waxes his skis so he can ski fast! He had 66 cans of ski wax. He used 49 cans of wax ~~and 26 waxing cloths.~~ (How many cans of wax are left?)

7. Last week the chairlift had 84 red chairs ~~and 22 green chairs.~~ This morning Bo saw a worker remove 16 red chairs. (How many red chairs are left?)

8. Bo Bunny had 56 different ski caps. He gave 17 of the ski caps to the bunnies in the beginning ski class. (How many ski caps does he have left?)

9. Bo began the day with 83¢. About midmorning he paid 57¢ for a mug of hot carrot juice. ~~His skiing buddy bought a turnip roll for 55¢.~~ (How much money does Bo have left?)

10. Hans Hare holds the record for the longest ski jump with a jump of 93 feet. ~~Bo Bunny jumped 70 feet on Thursday.~~ On Friday he jumped 77 feet. (To tie Hans's record, how many more feet does Bo need to jump?)

1.	2.	3.	4.	5.	6.	7.	8.	9.	10.
³12 4̶2̶ − 27 15	⁶15 $7̶5̶ − 29 $46	⁸14 9̶4̶ − 27 67	⁴10 5̶0̶ − 36 14	²15 3̶5̶ − 16 19	⁵16 6̶6̶ − 49 17	⁷14 8̶4̶ − 16 68	⁴16 5̶6̶ − 17 39	⁷13 8̶3̶¢ − 57 26 ¢	⁸13 9̶3̶ − 77 16

Name _____

A One-Of-A-Kind Pet Parade

Solve each problem. Show your work.
Cross out the matching answer in the answer bank.

a. 592 − 341	**b.** 543 − 232	**c.** 495 − 451	**d.** 897 − 567
e. 425 − 121	**f.** 736 − 612	**g.** 587 − 432	**h.** 864 − 452
i. 743 − 500	**j.** 839 − 633	**k.** 697 − 423	**l.** 956 − 753
m. 867 − 214	**n.** 981 − 771	**o.** 697 − 610	**p.** 549 − 228

Answer Bank

304
274
321
243
653
251
524
155
210
330
44
124
203
87
412
738
206
311

Bonus Box:
Use the two numbers left
in the answer bank to
write a subtraction problem.
Solve the problem
on the back!

Background For The Teacher
Pets

You name the animal and it's probably been a pet. People have tamed tigers, tarantulas, elephants, and other exotic creatures. By and large, however, humans confine their tastes to certain types of animals: dogs, cats, birds, fish, rodents, and reptiles/amphibians.

More than 150 million dogs live on earth, of which 30 million reside in the United States. Worldwide, there are 400 different dog pedigrees; within the United States, 100 pedigrees. Dogs have been useful to humans during their estimated 10,000-year association: they hunt, guard, race, guide visually impaired people, track missing people, and even search for illegal drugs.

Cats, on the other hand, have only been domesticated for 4,000 years. Long-haired Persians and shorthairs are the two basic categories of cats.

The interest in birds as pets is surging, despite severe import restrictions on some of the more exotic types. Birds of all types are good pets because of their singing, talking, and affectionate natures.

Fish are widely popular pets, too. They're modestly priced and easily cared for. Fish differ dramatically in appearance, swimming habits, and even in personalities.

Domesticated rodents are common pets. Pets within this family are white rats, guinea pigs, mice, hamsters, and gerbils. These animals are generally curious, intelligent, and fast to reproduce. Rabbits, though technically not rodents, are similar in these characteristics.

Answer Key

a. 251
b. 311
c. 44
d. 330
e. 304
f. 124
g. 155
h. 412
i. 243
j. 206
k. 274
l. 203
m. 653
n. 210
o. 87
p. 321

Bonus Box Answer:

$$738 - 524 = 214$$

Name _____

A Colorful Companion

Solve the problems. Show your work.
Color by the code.

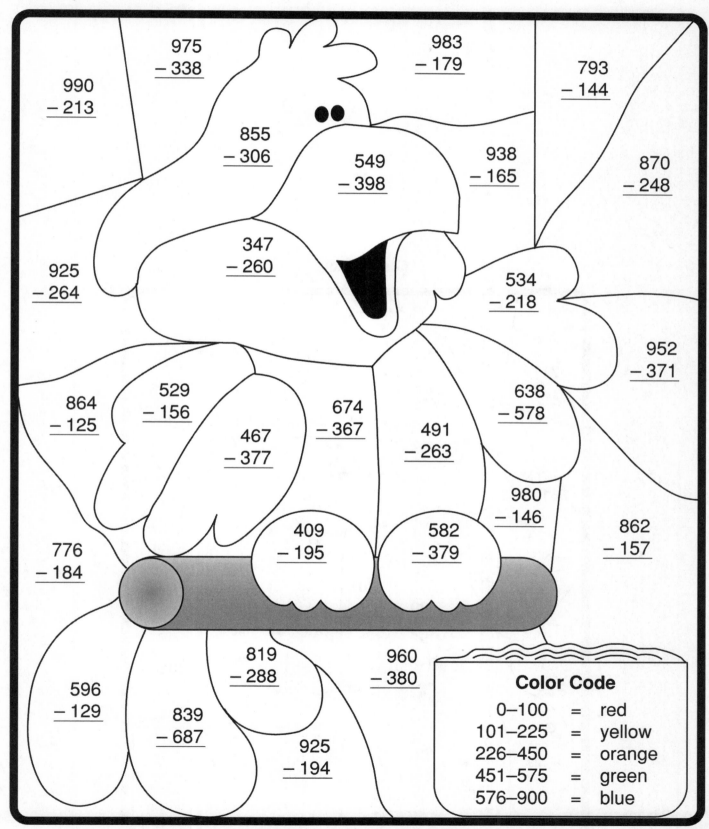

975
− 338

983
− 179

793
− 144

990
− 213

855
− 306

549
− 398

938
− 165

870
− 248

925
− 264

347
− 260

534
− 218

952
− 371

864
− 125

529
− 156

674
− 367

638
− 578

467
− 377

491
− 263

980
− 146

862
− 157

776
− 184

409
− 195

582
− 379

596
− 129

819
− 288

960
− 380

839
− 687

925
− 194

Color Code

0–100	=	red
101–225	=	yellow
226–450	=	orange
451–575	=	green
576–900	=	blue

Answer Key

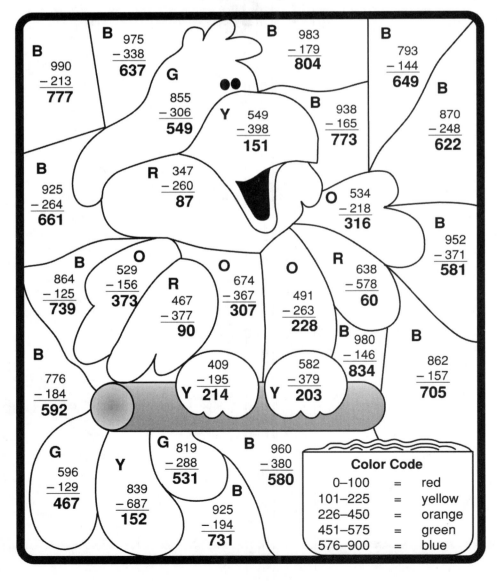

B
990
− 213
777

B 975
− 338
637

G 855
− 306
549

B 983
− 179
804

B 793
− 144
649

Y 549
− 398
151

B 938
− 165
773

B 870
− 248
622

B
925
− 264
661

R 347
− 260
87

O 534
− 218
316

B 952
− 371
581

B 864
− 125
739

O 529
− 156
373

R 467
− 377
90

O 674
− 367
307

O 491
− 263
228

R 638
− 578
60

B
776
− 184
592

Y 409
− 195
214

Y 582
− 379
203

B 980
− 146
834

B 862
− 157
705

G
596
− 129
467

Y
839
− 687
152

G 819
− 288
531

B 960
− 380
580

B 925
− 194
731

Color Code		
0–100	=	red
101–225	=	yellow
226–450	=	orange
451–575	=	green
576–900	=	blue

Fishy Friends

Solve each problem. Show your work.
If the answer on the fish is correct, color the fish.
If the answer is incorrect, copy and answer the problem on a blank fish.
Color, cut out, and glue that fish on top of the incorrect one.

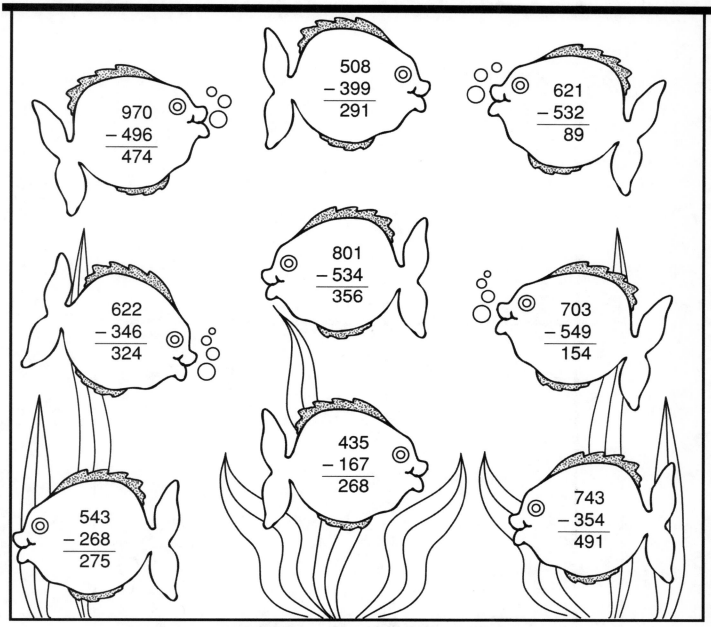

$$970 - 496 = 474$$

$$508 - 399 = 291$$

$$621 - 532 = 89$$

$$622 - 346 = 324$$

$$801 - 534 = 356$$

$$703 - 549 = 154$$

$$543 - 268 = 275$$

$$435 - 167 = 268$$

$$743 - 354 = 491$$

©The Education Center, Inc. • *The Best of* Teacher's Helper® *Math* • TEC3212

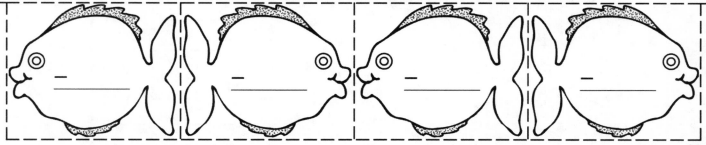

Answer Key

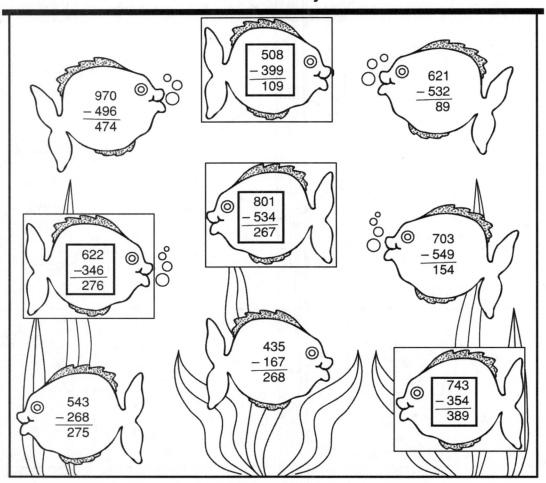

$$\begin{array}{r} 970 \\ -\ 496 \\ \hline 474 \end{array}$$

$$\begin{array}{r} 508 \\ -\ 399 \\ \hline 109 \end{array}$$

$$\begin{array}{r} 621 \\ -\ 532 \\ \hline 89 \end{array}$$

$$\begin{array}{r} 622 \\ -346 \\ \hline 276 \end{array}$$

$$\begin{array}{r} 801 \\ -\ 534 \\ \hline 267 \end{array}$$

$$\begin{array}{r} 703 \\ -\ 549 \\ \hline 154 \end{array}$$

$$\begin{array}{r} 543 \\ -\ 268 \\ \hline 275 \end{array}$$

$$\begin{array}{r} 435 \\ -\ 167 \\ \hline 268 \end{array}$$

$$\begin{array}{r} 743 \\ -\ 354 \\ \hline 389 \end{array}$$

Name _____

Huggable Hamsters

Solve the problems. Show your work.
Color the answers in the maze.

4	3	4								3	7	7		

6

| 1 | | 4 | 4 | 8 | | 1 | 0 | 6 | | 9 | 5 | | 1 |

| 9 | | | | | | | | | | | | | 5 |

$$705 - 536 \qquad 829 - 734 \qquad 2 \qquad 625 - 278 \qquad 894 - 537 \qquad 305 - 199 \qquad 713 - 453 \qquad 1$$

				4

| | | | | 7 |

| 3 | | | | | | | | | | | |
| 4 | $407 - 219$ | $238 - 145$ | | $702 - 325$ | $542 - 254$ | $914 - 763$ | $601 - 503$ | 2 |

| 7 | | | 2 | | | | | 6 |

| | | | 9 | | | | | 0 |

| 2 | $906 - 607$ | $573 - 125$ | 9 | $601 - 354$ | | 3 | 5 | 7 | |

| 8 | | | | | 1 |

| 8 | | | | | 8 | | | 1 |

| | | | | | 8 | | | 5 |

| 9 | $600 - 446$ | $608 - 174$ | $857 - 238$ | $340 - 218$ | | | | 4 |

| 8 |

| 9 | 3 | | | | | 1 | 2 | 2 | | 1 | 6 | 9 |

Answer Key

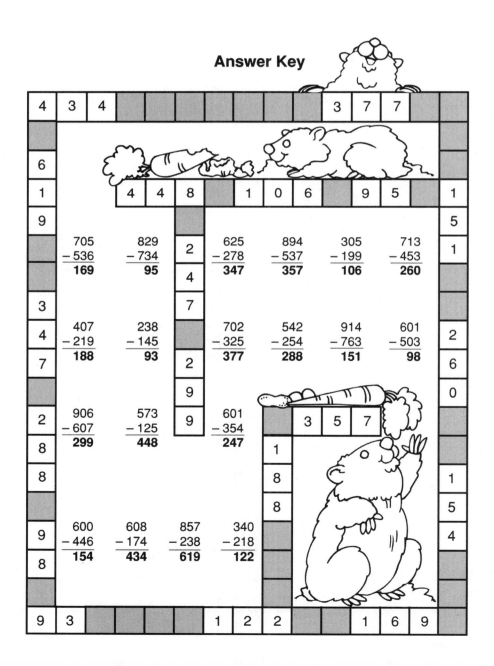

Border numbers (top, left-to-right): 4 3 4 ... 3 7 7

Left column (top to bottom): 6, 1, 9, 3, 4, 7, 2, 8, 8, 9, 8

Right column (top to bottom): 1, 5, 1, 2, 6, 0, 1, 5, 4

Inner top row: 4 4 8 ... 1 0 6 ... 9 5

Bottom row: 9 3 ... 1 2 2 ... 1 6 9

$$\begin{array}{r} 705 \\ -\,536 \\ \hline \mathbf{169} \end{array} \qquad \begin{array}{r} 829 \\ -\,734 \\ \hline \mathbf{95} \end{array} \qquad \begin{array}{r} 625 \\ -\,278 \\ \hline \mathbf{347} \end{array} \qquad \begin{array}{r} 894 \\ -\,537 \\ \hline \mathbf{357} \end{array} \qquad \begin{array}{r} 305 \\ -\,199 \\ \hline \mathbf{106} \end{array} \qquad \begin{array}{r} 713 \\ -\,453 \\ \hline \mathbf{260} \end{array}$$

Column between: 2, 4, 7

$$\begin{array}{r} 407 \\ -\,219 \\ \hline \mathbf{188} \end{array} \qquad \begin{array}{r} 238 \\ -\,145 \\ \hline \mathbf{93} \end{array} \qquad \begin{array}{r} 702 \\ -\,325 \\ \hline \mathbf{377} \end{array} \qquad \begin{array}{r} 542 \\ -\,254 \\ \hline \mathbf{288} \end{array} \qquad \begin{array}{r} 914 \\ -\,763 \\ \hline \mathbf{151} \end{array} \qquad \begin{array}{r} 601 \\ -\,503 \\ \hline \mathbf{98} \end{array}$$

Column between: 2, 9, 9

$$\begin{array}{r} 906 \\ -\,607 \\ \hline \mathbf{299} \end{array} \qquad \begin{array}{r} 573 \\ -\,125 \\ \hline \mathbf{448} \end{array} \qquad \begin{array}{r} 601 \\ -\,354 \\ \hline \mathbf{247} \end{array}$$

3 5 7

Inner right column: 1, 8, 8

$$\begin{array}{r} 600 \\ -\,446 \\ \hline \mathbf{154} \end{array} \qquad \begin{array}{r} 608 \\ -\,174 \\ \hline \mathbf{434} \end{array} \qquad \begin{array}{r} 857 \\ -\,238 \\ \hline \mathbf{619} \end{array} \qquad \begin{array}{r} 340 \\ -\,218 \\ \hline \mathbf{122} \end{array}$$

Name _____

How Many Miles?

Use the mileage code.
Complete the table.

Mileage Code

X = 10   ▲ = 1

City	Miles To Reach The City	Tens	Ones
Foursfield	X X X X ▲ ▲ ▲ ▲ ▲	4	5
Threesburg	X X ▲ ▲ ▲ ▲ ▲ ▲ ▲		
Onesboro	▲ ▲ ▲ ▲ ▲ ▲ ▲ ▲ ▲		
Nine City	X X X X ▲ ▲ ▲ ▲		
Eight Creek	X X X X X X X X		
Twos Town	X ▲ ▲ ▲ ▲ ▲		
Fivesville	X X X ▲ ▲ ▲ ▲ ▲ ▲		
Sixco	X X X X X ▲ ▲		
Sevenland	X X X X X X ▲ ▲ ▲		
Tenwick	X X ▲ ▲ ▲ ▲		

Use the table to complete the road sign.

On each line write how many miles must be traveled to reach the city.

Road Sign

Onesboro	_____ miles	Sixco	_____ miles
Twos Town	_____ miles	Sevenland	_____ miles
Threesburg	_____ miles	Eight Creek	_____ miles
Foursfield	45 miles	Nine City	_____ miles
Fivesville	_____ miles	Tenwick	_____ miles

Bonus Box: The last stop for this bus is Eight Creek. On the back of this paper, list the order in which the bus will reach the cities listed on the sign. (Hint: Begin your list with Onesboro and end it with Eight Creek.)

How To Use This Place-Value Unit
Pages 35–44

The reproducibles in this unit are designed to assess or reinforce your students' place-value skills. The activities can be used collectively or independently at any time of the school year.

Extension Activities

— Keep your students' appetites for place-value practice on track with this tasty activity! Provide each student with a napkin, a whole graham cracker that is visually divided into fourths, and a handful of miniature marshmallows. Have each student break apart the four sections of her graham cracker and arrange them in columns side by side. Explain that these sections will represent the place-value columns of thousands, hundreds, tens, and ones. Then instruct the students to place a designated number of marshmallows in each of the four columns. After the graham crackers are loaded, have the students recite the number they have created (such as "Four thousand, three hundred, eighty-five"). Repeat the activity a desired number of times—having students create a different number each time. Conclude the activity by inviting students to eat their cracker and marshmallow manipulatives!

— These student-made, suitcase-shaped folders are perfect for storing and transporting completed place-value activities! To make a folder:
1. Fold a 12" x 18" sheet of construction paper in half. Position the fold at the bottom; then staple the sides of the project to create a large pocket.
2. Fold a 4 1/2" x 10" strip of construction paper in half. Cut two matching suitcase handles from the folded paper. Securely glue the ends of the handles inside the folded project as shown—one handle per side.
3. Personalize the resulting suitcase and add desired decorations using crayons, markers, or construction-paper scraps.

Throughout your place-value studies, have students store their completed activities in their personalized suitcase folders. When a desired number of activities has been completed and packed for transport, students can proudly carry home their personalized travel bags.

Finished Project

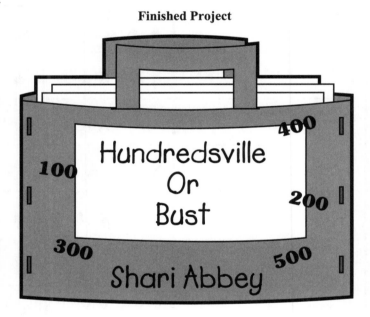

Answer Key

Tens	Ones
4	5
2	7
	9
4	4
8	0
1	5
3	6
5	2
6	3
2	4

Road Sign

Onesboro	9	miles	Sixco	52	miles
Twos Town	15	miles	Sevenland	63	miles
Threesburg	27	miles	Eight Creek	80	miles
Foursfield	45	miles	Nine City	44	miles
Fivesville	36	miles	Tenwick	24	miles

Bonus Box Answer:
Onesboro
Twos Town
Tenwick
Threesburg
Fivesville
Nine City
Foursfield
Sixco
Sevenland
Eight Creek

Name_____

A Place To Stay

Name the place value of each underlined digit.
Write the room key number on the matching building.

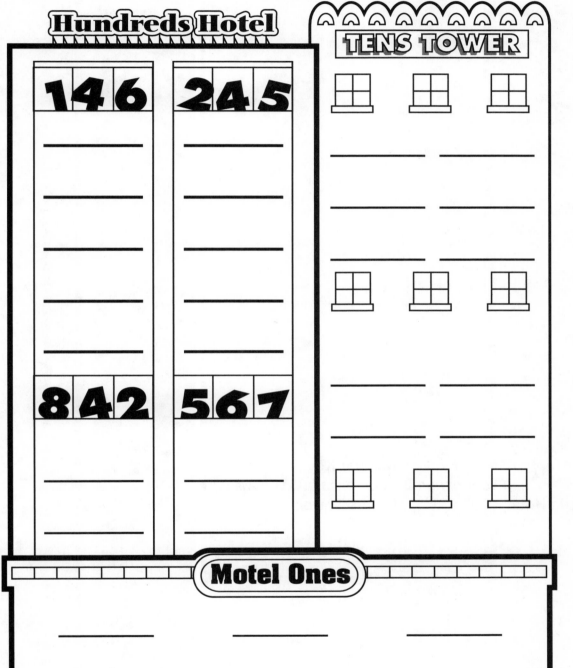

Room Key Numbers

74<u>2</u>
<u>2</u>19
3<u>8</u>
<u>1</u>06
78<u>1</u>
<u>2</u>4
45<u>5</u>
<u>6</u>97
36<u>3</u>
5<u>6</u>0
<u>5</u>54
<u>3</u>07
8<u>3</u>5
<u>7</u>2
92<u>6</u>
<u>2</u>41
47<u>9</u>
1<u>1</u>0
<u>8</u>08
6<u>3</u>3
<u>9</u>24
<u>5</u>90
78<u>8</u>
2<u>1</u>7
<u>9</u>95
8<u>6</u>2
<u>5</u>1
<u>3</u>43
17<u>6</u>
<u>4</u>89
<u>5</u>8
93<u>3</u>
<u>1</u>24
<u>7</u>5

37

Answer Key
(Order of numbers on each building will vary.)

Hundreds Hotel	Tens Tower	Motel Ones
219	24	742
106	560	38
697	835	781
554	72	455
995	110	363
862	633	926
489	217	479
307	51	788
241	58	176
808	933	75
924		
590		
343		
124		

Name_____

All Aboard!

Use the numerals boarding each bus to make six numbers.
Write the numbers on the lines.

Draw a purple circle around the largest
number on each bus.
Draw a green box around the smallest
number on each bus.

Bonus Box: Ready for a challenge? Choose four different numerals from 1 to 9. On the back of this paper, use
the numerals to make as many different four-digit numbers as you can! Draw a purple circle around the largest
number you make. Draw a green box around the smallest
number you make. (Can you make 24 different numbers?)

Answer Key
(Order of numbers on each bus will vary.)

Numeral World
316
361
136
163
613
631

Mount Million
842
824
284
248
482
428

Digit Falls
675
657
576
567
765
756

House Of Numbers
189
198
981
918
819
891

Addition Stadium
493
439
349
394
934
943

Calculator Fair
526
562
625
652
265
256

Name_____

Off to Hundredsville!
Place value: ones through thousands

Picture-Perfect Places

Use the information in each picture frame to make a number.
Write each number on the matching line below.

A.
9 ones
2 thousands
3 tens
5 hundreds

B.
1 hundred
4 thousands
0 tens
6 ones

C.
7 tens
2 ones
9 hundreds
1 thousand

D.
5 thousands
2 hundreds
5 ones
8 tens

E.
5 tens
4 hundreds
9 thousands
8 ones

F.
7 hundreds
2 tens
3 thousands
1 one

G.
7 thousands
8 hundreds
6 tens
3 ones

H.
0 ones
6 hundreds
4 tens
8 thousands

I.
3 hundreds
1 ten
4 ones
6 thousands

J.
9 tens
7 ones
3 thousands
1 hundred

K.
5 ones
0 tens
0 hundreds
5 thousands

L.
1 thousand
3 ones
7 tens
2 hundreds

M.
3 tens
9 thousands
2 ones
6 hundreds

N.
9 hundreds
4 thousands
8 ones
5 tens

Number Box

A. _____   H. _____

B. _____   I. _____

C. _____   J. _____

D. _____   K. _____

E. _____   L. _____

F. _____   M. _____

G. _____   N. _____

Welcome to
Digit Falls

Bonus Box: On the back of this paper, write the numbers in the Number Box in order from smallest to largest.

Answer Key

A.	2,539	**H.**	8,640
B.	4,106	**I.**	6,314
C.	1,972	**J.**	3,197
D.	5,285	**K.**	5,005
E.	9,458	**L.**	1,273
F.	3,721	**M.**	9,632
G.	7,863	**N.**	4,958

Bonus Box Answers:

1,273
1,972
2,539
3,197
3,721
4,106
4,958
5,005
5,285
6,314
7,863
8,640
9,458
9,632

Name _____

Going Places!

Materials needed: One game sheet and pencil per student, one die per pair

Directions for each round:
1. Player 1 rolls the die and calls out the number that is rolled.
2. Each player chooses a box and writes that number in it.
3. Player 2 rolls the die and calls out the number that is rolled.
4. Each player chooses a box and writes that number in it.
5. Repeat steps 1 through 4 to finish the round.
6. In turn each player writes the points for that round in the Point Box.
   Higher number = *2 points*
   Lower number = *1 point*
   Player correctly reads his or her number aloud = *1 point*

Game One: Numeral World

Point Box

Round 1

Round 2

Round 3

Game Two: Addition Stadium

Point Box

Round 1

Round 2

Round 3

Game Three: Mount Million

Point Box

Round 1

Round 2

Round 3

Bonus Box: Add the points in each Point Box. If you earned more than five points at one place, color the corresponding picture!

How To Use Page 43

If desired, introduce this game of chance and strategy by playing a practice round as a class activity. On the chalkboard draw a set of four boxes (with a comma) as shown on page 43. Ask each child to draw a similar set of boxes on a piece of scrap paper. Roll a die and call out the number rolled. Instruct each child to write this number in one box on his paper. Tell students that the object of the game is to create the largest number possible. Also inform students that once a number has been written, it cannot be erased. Continue with three more rolls of the die so that each player's boxes are filled. Invite each child to read aloud the number he created, thus earning one point each. Then award those students who created the largest possible number two points each and the students who created the smallest possible number one point each. Next distribute student copies of page 43. Answer any questions about the practice round of play before pairing students for this fun-filled place-value activity.

Name _____

Time For A Snack

Write the time on the lines below each clock.
Color the cheese holes yellow as you use the answers.

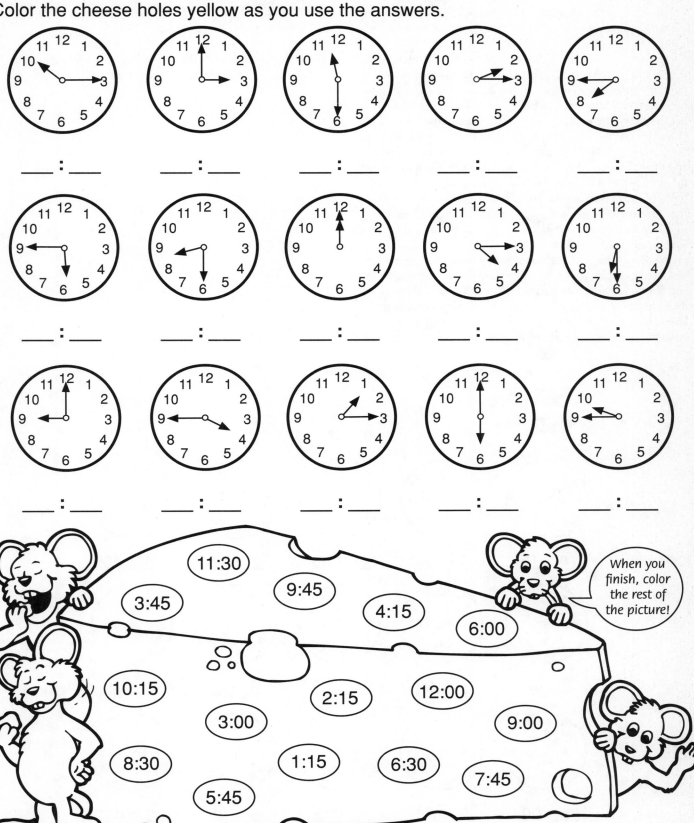

___ : ___   ___ : ___   ___ : ___   ___ : ___   ___ : ___

___ : ___   ___ : ___   ___ : ___   ___ : ___   ___ : ___

___ : ___   ___ : ___   ___ : ___   ___ : ___   ___ : ___

11:30
9:45
4:15
6:00
3:45
10:15
2:15
12:00
3:00
9:00
8:30
1:15
6:30
7:45
5:45

When you finish, color the rest of the picture!

Background For The Teacher
Time And Clocks

Long ago people could tell how much time had passed by watching the sun. Shadow clocks, water clocks, sand clocks, burning candles, and rope clocks were invented to keep track of passing time. Mechanical clocks began to appear in the late 1200s. Minute and second hands were common by the early 1700s.

The sun's placement in the sky was used to set the time on the first individual clocks. This resulted in few clocks showing the same time. The invention of the time ball (a large, hollow, red, metal ball attached to a high pole and lowered at noon) helped people living in the same town synchronize their times. However, this did not help people from town to town agree on the time of day. This was a serious problem for the railroads and their passengers. On November 18, 1883, the railroad took the suggestion of Charles Dowd and established a standard time for the United States. This divided the United States into four time zones, and clocks were set accordingly. Congress legalized this system in 1918. Though altered, these time zones are still in effect today.

In nature time is kept without the use of a clock. Roosters wake up and crow at sunrise every morning. Some oysters open and close their shells as the tides change. Various plants open their flowers at certain times of the day or night. Scientists know that living organisms have a method of telling time and continue to search for new information and explanations.

Book Corner
Time And Clocks

Tick-Tock • Written by Eileen Browne & Illustrated by David Parkins • Candlewick Press, 1996

Clocks And More Clocks • Written & Illustrated by Pat Hutchins • Aladdin Paperbacks, 1994

The Grouchy Ladybug • Written & Illustrated by Eric Carle • HarperCollins Children's Books, 1996

Answer Key

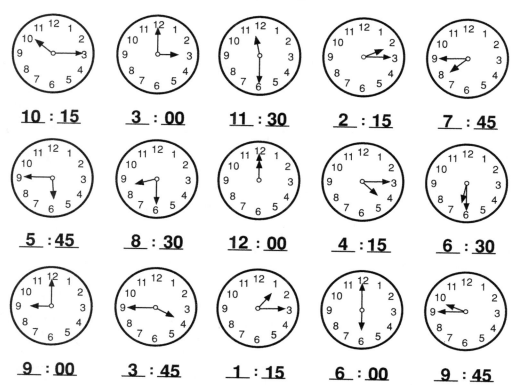

Name _____

Mice
Time word problems
to five minutes

Perfect Timing

Read each problem.
Write the time on the lines.
Draw the hands on the clock to match.

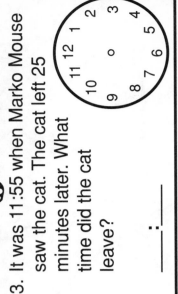

1. Morris Mouse put a cheese pie in the oven at 3:25. The pie must bake for 40 minutes. What time will the pie be done?

___:___

2. Mia Mouse is going to visit Rita Rat. It takes 55 minutes to scurry to Rita's place. It is 8:20 now. What time will Mia get there?

___:___

3. It was 11:55 when Marko Mouse saw the cat. The cat left 25 minutes later. What time did the cat leave?

___:___

4. Mindy is expecting a visitor in a half hour. It is 9:10 now. If the visitor is on time, when will she arrive?

___:___

5. It was 6:40 when Morris started feeling hungry. He didn't eat breakfast for 1 hour and 20 minutes. What time was breakfast?

___:___

6. Marko called in his pizza order at 12:05. The pizza arrived 45 minutes later. What time was the pizza delivered?

___:___

7. At 4:30 Mia started exercising. She worked out for one hour and five minutes. What time did she quit?

___:___

8. Max is always 15 minutes late! The party started at 7:30. What time will Max get to the party?

___:___

Bonus Box: Morris just took a cheese-cake out of the oven. It is 2:20. The cheesecake baked for 35 minutes. What time did Morris put the cake in the oven?

___:___

How To Use The Patterns On This Page

Using these adorable clock manipulatives, students can have the times of their lives solving the word problems on page 47. Each student needs a construction-paper copy of the patterns below, a brad, scissors, access to a hole puncher, and crayons or markers. Have each student color and cut out his patterns, then punch a hole at the dot on each clock hand. Demonstrate how to use a brad to attach the clock hands to the clock face (for ease in spinning, avoid attaching the brad too tightly), and provide assistance as needed. Hickory, dickory, dock—there's a mouse in that clock!

©The Education Center, Inc.

Answer Key
(Each clock should match its listed time.)

1. 4:05
2. 9:15
3. 12:20
4. 9:40
5. 8:00
6. 12:50
7. 5:35
8. 7:45

Bonus Box Answer: 1:45

Every Minute Counts

Complete the hands on the clocks.
Write the letter of the correct clock by each sentence.

a.

g.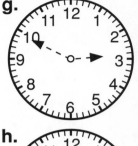

_____ Moe wakes up every morning at <u>6:37</u>.

_____ At <u>7:22</u> he eats a bowl of Cheese Flakes for breakfast.

_____ The cat snoops around the front door at about <u>8:29</u>.

b.

h.

_____ By <u>9:06</u> Moe has scurried off to Squeak School.

_____ Safety class begins at <u>10:43</u>.

c.

i.

_____ When lunch is served at <u>11:55</u>, he's very hungry.

_____ All the mice play until <u>12:12</u>.

_____ School is out at <u>2:49</u>.

d.

j.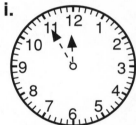

_____ Moe meets his friends for a game of tag at <u>3:09</u>.

_____ By <u>4:20</u> Moe is ready for a snack.

_____ Moe helps set the table for dinner at <u>5:38</u>.

e.

k.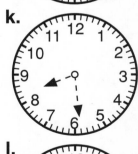

_____ By <u>7:39</u> Moe has finished his homework.

f.

l.

Bonus Box: On the back of this sheet, draw a clock that shows your favorite time of the day. Draw and color a picture that shows what you do at that time.

Answer Key

c
h
k
a
f
i
d
g
e
j
l
b

Who's Got The Time?

A Matching Game

Write a different time on each piece of cheese.
On the clock beside the cheese, show that time.

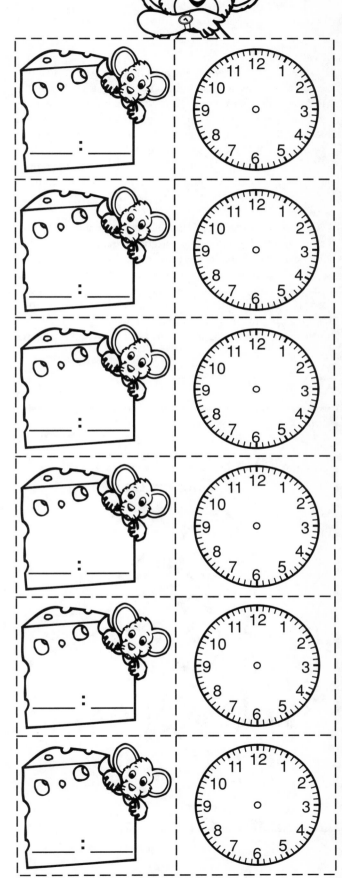

Materials Needed For Each Student

— pencil
— scissors
— resealable plastic bag
— construction-paper copy of title card (below)

How To Use Page 51

Have students complete the activity on page 51; then pair youngsters and ask each child to check his partner's paper. After the papers have been returned to their original owners and corrected (if necessary), have each student personalize a title card. Then have each student cut out his game pieces and title card and store them in a plastic bag. Set aside time for students to trade game bags and complete several matching activities that their classmates have created. At the end of the allotted time, have students return the games to their original owners.

Or pair the students and ask that they play with only one of their card sets. To play a concentration-type game, have the students in each pair shuffle the cards in one set and place each card facedown on a playing surface. In turn, each child turns over two cards. If the cards show the same time, the child keeps the cards and turns over two more cards. If the cards don't match, the child turns them facedown again. Play continues in the same manner. The child with the most cards at the end of the game wins.

Title Cards

Name_____

Who's Got The Time?
A Matching Game

Name_____

Who's Got The Time?
A Matching Game

Name _____

Boot Loot

Count the money on each boot.
Write the amount on the boot's spur.
Color the boot in each pair that has more money.

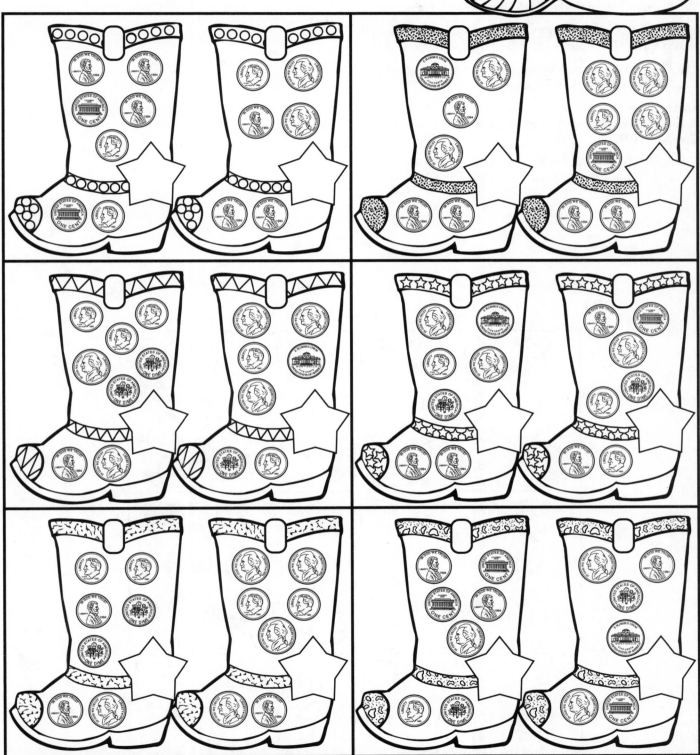

Book Corner
Money
Fiction

Alexander, Who Used To Be Rich Last Sunday • Written by Judith Viorst & Illustrated by Ray Cruz • Aladdin Paperbacks, 1980

If You Made A Million • Written by David M. Schwartz & Illustrated by Steven Kellogg • Mulberry Books, 1994

Four Dollars And Fifty Cents • Written by Eric A. Kimmel & Illustrated by Glen Rounds • Holiday House, Inc.; 1993

The Money Tree • Written by Sarah Stewart & Illustrated by David Small • Farrar, Straus & Giroux, Inc.; 1991

Max Malone Makes A Million • Written by Charlotte Herman & Illustrated by Cat Bowman Smith • Henry Holt And Company, 1992

Picking Peas For A Penny • Written by Angela Shelf Medearis & Illustrated by Charles G. Shaw • Scholastic Inc., 1993

Nonfiction

The Story Of Money • Written by Betsy Maestro & Illustrated by Giulio Maestro • Mulberry Books, 1995

Money, Money, Money: The Meaning Of The Art And Symbols On U.S. Paper Currency • Written & Illustrated by Nancy Winslow Parker • HarperCollins Children's Books, 1995

Answer Key

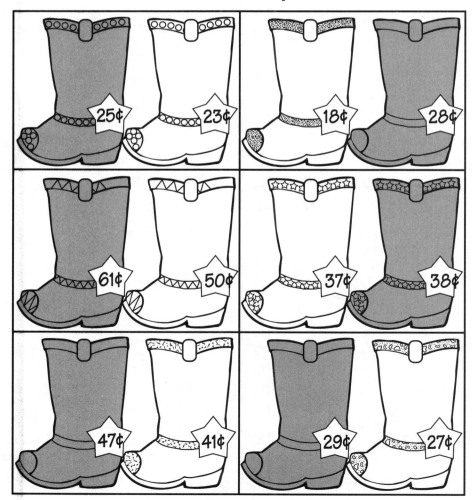

Name _____

Cactus Cash

Count the money in each row.
Write the amount on the cactus.
Color the matching star.

52¢ 66¢ 58¢ 97¢ 91¢ 85¢ 86¢ 69¢ 67¢

A. ___¢

B. ___¢

C. ___¢

D. ___¢

E. ___¢

F. ___¢

G. ___¢

H. ___¢

Bonus:
Find the star you did not color. Write that amount on the back of this page. Draw and color five coins that equal the amount. Color the star.

Award

Duplicate and present this award to your students to acknowledge their success with money skills.

This
Buckaroo Award

goes to

_____

for outstanding performance
with money skills!

_____
Signed

_____
Date

Answer Key
A. 97¢
B. 85¢
C. 67¢
D. 91¢
E. 69¢
F. 58¢
G. 86¢
H. 52¢

Bonus Box Answer: 66¢: 2 quarters, 1 dime, 1 nickel, 1 penny

Name _____

Chow Time!

Chow down at Charlie's Chuckwagon.
Write the amount of money you have in the blank.
Subtract the cost of the item you buy.
Color the amount of money you have left.

Money You Have	You Buy	Money You Have Left
A. $_____.___	Beef Stew 69¢	
B. $_____.___	Baked Beans 56¢	
C. $_____.___	Peach Cobbler 44¢	
D. $_____.___	Rattlesnake Nuggets 85¢	
E. $_____.___	Chili 79¢	
F. $_____.___	Fluffy Biscuit 38¢	
G. $_____.___	Barbecue Sandwich 90¢	

Answer Key

A.	$	.80	nickel, nickel, penny
B.	$	.86	quarter, nickel
C.	$	.76	quarter, nickel, penny, penny
D.	$	.95	nickel, nickel
E.	$	.95	nickel, nickel, nickel, penny
F.	$	.46	nickel, penny, penny, penny
G.	$	.90	no change

Good Horse "Cents"

Price List

one horseshoe .... $ .43	saddle wax .... $ .25
bucket of oats .... $ .32	short rope .... $ .31
bale of hay .... $ .66	long rope .... $ .57

Use the Price List to help you solve the problems.
Show your work in the boxes below.
Write your answers on the lines.

1. How much will it cost to buy saddle wax and a short rope?   1._____

2. If you have 99¢, how much money will you have left after you   2._____
   buy two horseshoes?

3. Can you buy a bucket of oats and a bale of hay with 95¢?   3._____

4. Will three quarters buy a bale of hay?   4._____

5. Would it cost less to buy two short ropes or one long rope?   5._____

6. You need to buy one horseshoe, a short rope, and saddle wax.   6._____
   How much money do you need?

7. How much more does a bale of hay cost than a bucket of oats?   7._____

8. Will $2.00 buy four new horseshoes for your horse?   8._____

Bonus Box: A person who has good *horse sense* has *common sense.* What do you think common sense is? Do you think you have good horse sense? Why or why not? Write your answers on the back of this page.

1.	2.	3.	4.
5.	6.	7.	8.

Answer Key

1. 56¢
2. 13¢
3. no
4. yes
5. one long rope
6. 99¢
7. 34¢
8. yes

A Rootin'-Tootin' Sale

Cut out the prices.
Read the Cowpoke Clues.
Glue the prices in place.

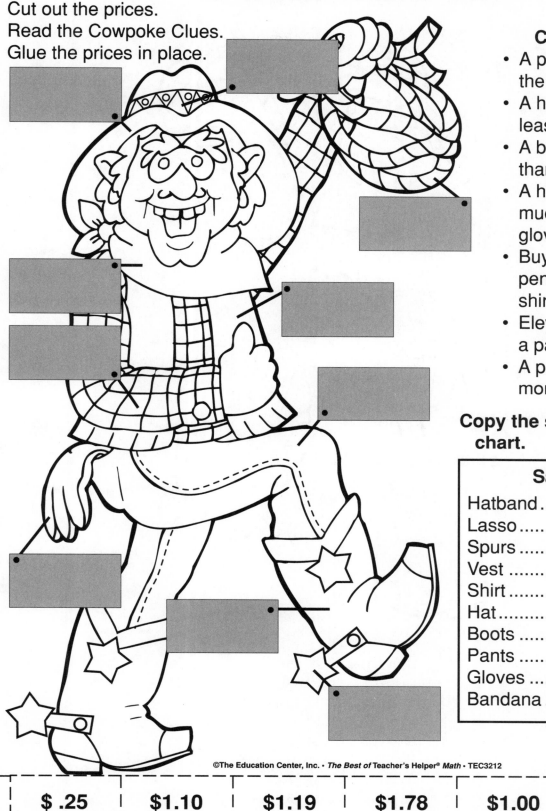

Cowpoke Clues

- A pair of boots costs the most.
- A hatband costs the least.
- A bandana costs less than 50¢.
- A hat costs twice as much as a pair of gloves.
- Buy a lasso, or for a penny more, buy a shirt.
- Eleven dimes will buy a pair of spurs.
- A pair of pants costs more than a vest.

Copy the sale prices on the chart.

Sale Prices

Hatband	$ ____.____
Lasso	$ ____.____
Spurs	$ ____.____
Vest	$ ____.____
Shirt	$ ____.____
Hat	$ ____.____
Boots	$ ____.____
Pants	$ ____.____
Gloves	$ ____.____
Bandana	$ ____.____

©The Education Center, Inc. • *The Best of* Teacher's Helper® *Math* • TEC3212

$ .25	$1.10	$1.19	$1.78	$1.00
$1.20	$1.67	$2.00	$ .49	$2.16

Bonus Box:
What four items could you buy for exactly $4.00? Write your answer on the back of this page.

61

Answer Key

$2.00

$ .25

$1.19

$ .49

$1.67

$1.20

$1.78

$1.00

$2.16

$1.10

Hatband............	$ .25
Lasso...............	$1.19
Spurs	$1.10
Vest	$1.67
Shirt	$1.20
Hat...................	$2.00
Boots	$2.16
Pants	$1.78
Gloves	$1.00
Bandana	$ .49

Bonus Box Answer: spurs, boots, hatband, bandana

Name _____

Floating Fortunes

Count the coins on each balloon.
Write the amount in the blank.
Color the balloon in each pair that shows more money.

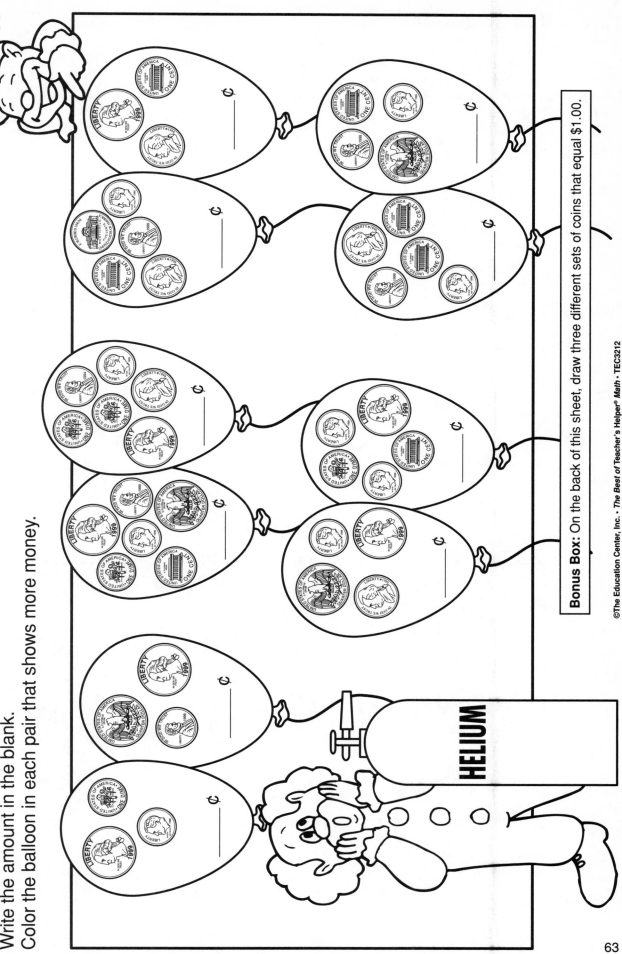

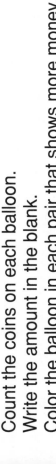

Bonus Box: On the back of this sheet, draw three different sets of coins that equal $1.00.

How To Use This Money Unit
Pages 63–72

Use this rich collection of activities to reinforce and assess your students' understanding of money. Your youngsters are sure to cash in on a wealth of knowledge as they clown around with their money skills!

Answer Key

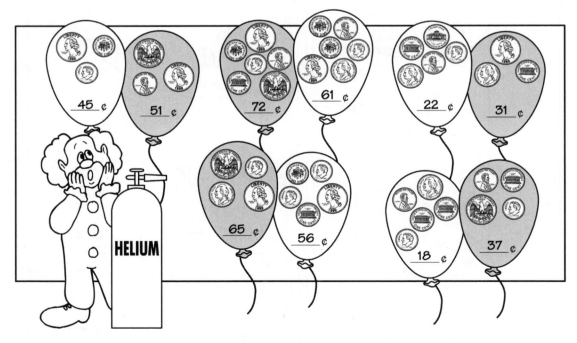

Bonus Box Answer: Answers will vary.

Name_____

The Juggling Act

Get in on the juggling act!
Cut out the coins below.
Juggle the coins to match the amount shown on each clown's hat.
Then glue each set of five coins in place.

Clara Clown

56¢

Clyde Clown

95¢

Calvin Clown

13¢

Carla Clown

85¢

Bonus Box: After the show, Clyde Clown is going to use his money to go shopping. On the back of this sheet, make a list of five items that may cost less than 95¢.

©The Education Center, Inc. • *The Best of* Teacher's Helper® *Math* • TEC3212

Answer Key

(Arrangement of coins will vary.)

Clara Clown 56¢

Clyde Clown 95¢

Calvin Clown 13¢

Carla Clown 85¢

Bonus Box Answer: Answers will vary.

Name_____

Gearing Up for the Show

Which coins should these clever clowns use to pay for their clown gear?
Use pennies, nickels, dimes, or quarters to find out.
Write your answers on the chart.
The first one is done for you.

Items for Sale	How can the item be purchased...	How can the item be purchased...
bow tie 17¢	with 5 coins? *3 nickels* *2 pennies*	with 8 coins?
clown hat 25¢	with 5 coins?	with 7 coins?
clown hair 77¢	with 5 coins?	with 7 coins?
clown shoes 86¢	with 5 coins?	with 7 coins?
makeup kit 55¢	with 4 coins?	with 7 coins?

Bonus Box: Why is it sometimes better to pay for items with bills instead of coins? Write your answer on the back of this sheet.

Materials Needed For Each Student
— play money coins or a copy of the coin patterns on page 72
— a resealable plastic bag (optional)

How To Use Page 67
1. Provide each youngster with a copy of page 67 and the materials listed on this page. If necessary, provide each student with scissors to cut out her coin patterns.
2. Have each student manipulate her coins to complete the activity as directed.
3. If desired, have each student store her coins in a resealable plastic bag to later use with the extension activity on page 70.

Answer Key

Items for Sale	How can the item be purchased...	How can the item be purchased...
bow tie 17¢	with 5 coins? *3 nickels* *2 pennies*	with 8 coins? *1 dime* *7 pennies*
clown hat 25¢	with 5 coins? *5 nickels*	with 7 coins? *2 dimes* *5 pennies*
clown hair 77¢	with 5 coins? *3 quarters* *2 pennies*	with 7 coins? *2 quarters* *2 dimes* *1 nickel* *2 pennies*
clown shoes 86¢	with 5 coins? *3 quarters* *1 dime* *1 penny*	with 7 coins? *2 quarters* *3 dimes* *1 nickel* *1 penny*
makeup kit 55¢	with 4 coins? *1 quarter* *3 dimes*	with 7 coins? *2 quarters* *5 pennies or* *4 dimes* *3 nickels*

Bonus Box Answer: Students' answers will vary. But students should have written a sentence similar to the following: *If the item is expensive, it could take a large amount of coins to pay for it.*

Name_____

Clown Cafe

Each clown is thinking of a snack to buy at the cafe.
Find out how much each clown's snack will cost.
Show your work in each box.

ice cream	....	$.75	hot dog	....	$1.75
pretzel	....	$.65	hamburger	....	$2.25
popcorn	....	$.95	soda	....	$.45
cotton candy	....	$1.25	lemonade	....	$.85

CLOWN CAFE PRICES

A. Smiley

E. Slappy

B. Bobo

F. Jolly

C. Patches

G. Giggles

D. Lucky

H. Bonkers

Bonus Box: Each clown has $2.75 to spend. Which clowns will be able to buy the items they want at the cafe? Write their names on the back of this sheet.

Extension Activity

This coin exchange contest is sure to dazzle your youngsters as they each try to earn one dollar. Pair students and provide each twosome with a pile of play-money coins (16 pennies, 8 nickels, 4 dimes, 8 quarters) or use the coin manipulatives from page 72. Also give each pair a sharpened pencil, a copy of the clown spinner on this page, and a large paper clip.

To earn a dollar, a player spins the paper clip and collects the corresponding number of pennies from the coin pile. If possible, she then trades the pennies for equivalent coins. Her turn is over and the next player takes a turn. As each player accumulates coins, have her trade up for larger coins. The first player to accumulate four quarters strikes it rich and wins the game!

Clown Spinner

Assembled Project

Answer Key

A.	$ .75	B.	$ .85	C.	$1.75	D.	$ .75
	+ $ .95		$ .65		$1.25		$ .45
	$1.70		$1.50		$3.00		$1.20

E.	$2.25	F.	$2.25	G.	$1.75	H.	$ 2.25
	+ $1.25		$ .45		$ .75		$ .85
	$3.50		$2.70		$2.50		$ 3.10

Bonus Box Answer: Smiley, Bobo, Lucky, Jolly, and Giggles

Clown Capers

Solve each problem in order.
Show your work.
Write your answer on the line.
Color the cannonball with the matching answer.

POOF!

20¢ 75¢ 10¢
60¢ 50¢ 45¢ 80¢

A. Giggles has 25¢. How much more money will she need to buy a balloon that costs 45¢?

_____ ¢

B. Smiley has twice as much money as Giggles. How much money does she have?

_____ ¢

C. Jolly had 95¢ until she gave Slappy 4 nickels. How much money does she have left?

_____ ¢

D. Lucky has 1 dime, 1 quarter, and 10 pennies. How much money does he have in all?

_____ ¢

E. Bonkers gave Lucky 1 dime and 1 nickel. How much money does Lucky have now?

_____ ¢

F. Patches buys 8 small balloons for 10¢ each. How much does he pay in all?

_____ ¢

G. Bobo has 1 quarter and 5 dimes. She buys a 65¢ pretzel. How much does she have left?

_____ ¢

Bonus Box: On the back of this sheet, list your answers in order from least to greatest.

Manipulative Coin Patterns

Answer Key

A. 20¢
B. 50¢
C. 75¢
D. 45¢
E. 60¢
F. 80¢
G. 10¢

Bonus Box Answer: 10¢, 20¢, 45¢, 50¢, 60¢, 75¢, 80¢

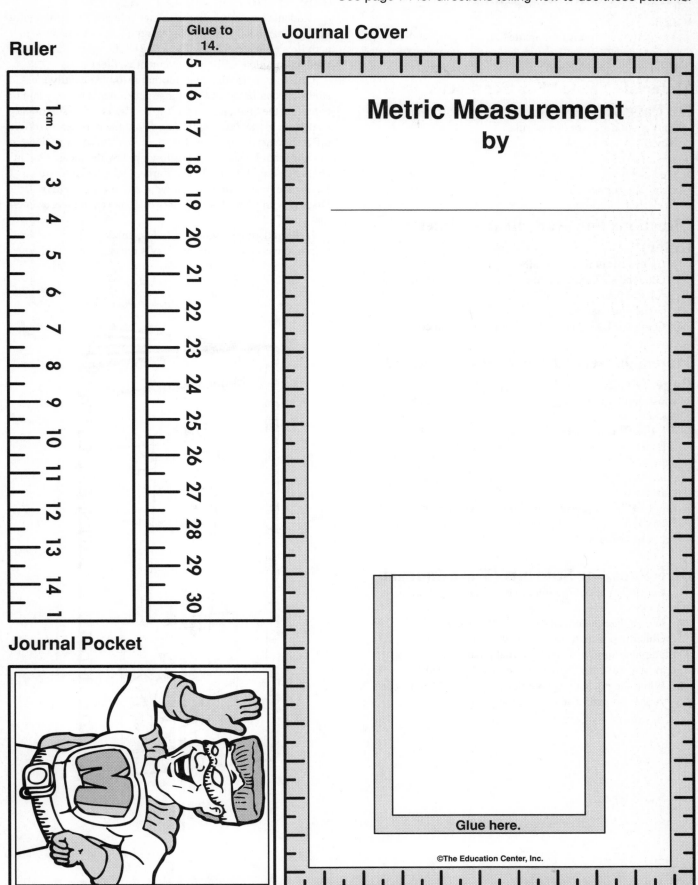

Ruler

Glue to 14.

Journal Cover

Metric Measurement
by

_____

Glue here.

©The Education Center, Inc.

Journal Pocket

How To Use This Metric Linear-Measurement Unit Pages 73–82

The activities in this unit are designed to give students plenty of hands-on practice with linear measurement.

Materials Needed For Centimeter Ruler On Page 73

— construction-paper copy of ruler
— pencil
— scissors
— glue
— clear tape (optional)

Directions For Students (Centimeter Ruler)

1. Carefully cut out each ruler section.
2. Glue the sections together where indicated. Allow the ruler to dry.
3. Write your name on the ruler.
4. Optional: Use clear tape to reinforce the glued area.

Materials Needed For Math Journal On Page 73

— construction-paper copy of journal cover and journal pocket
— 4 1/4" x 9" rectangle of construction paper (back cover)
— scissors
— pencil
— glue
— crayons
— supply of blank journal pages (approximately 4" x 8 1/2" each)
— access to a stapler

Directions For Students (Math Journal)

1. Carefully cut out the journal cover and the journal pocket.
2. Personalize the cover and color the pocket.
3. Glue the pocket to the cover where indicated.
4. Staple a supply of blank journal pages between your journal covers. (Provide assistance as needed.)
5. When the pocket has completely dried, fold and store your centimeter ruler inside the pocket.

How To Use The Centimeter Ruler And The Math Journal On Page 73

Students can use their centimeter rulers (or commercially made ones) to help them complete the linear-measurement activities on pages 75, 77, 79, and 81. The rulers can also be used to complete daily measurement challenges.

One way to use the math journal is to post a daily measurement challenge and then instruct students to copy and complete the challenge in their journals. The measurement challenge of the day might read, "Find the perimeters of five different classroom items. List the items and their perimeters in your math journal." The following day, the measurement challenge could read, "Trade journals with a classmate. Verify the measurements that were recorded yesterday. Discuss with your classmate any differences in measurement that you find."

If desired, at the end of each day, enlist your youngsters' help in creating the following day's measurement challenge.

Name _____

Go The Distance

Use a centimeter ruler. Start at the ★.
For each location:
  Measure each line segment.
  Write the measurement in the ◯.
  Add the numbers.
  Write the total length of the line in the ▭.

Metric Dome

Linears vs. Grams
8:00 tonight

cm

High Flyers School

cm

Today's class:
How To Make A
Perfect Landing

CENTIMETER CINEMA

NOW SHOWING
**METRIC MAN GOES
TO HOLLYWOOD**

cm

MacMeasures

Burgers that
measure up!

cm

cm

Bonus Box: In the empty box, draw another place that Metric Man might like to visit. Draw and measure line segments from the ★ to the ●. Do not cross any lines. Write the total length of the line in the ▭ .

Answer Key

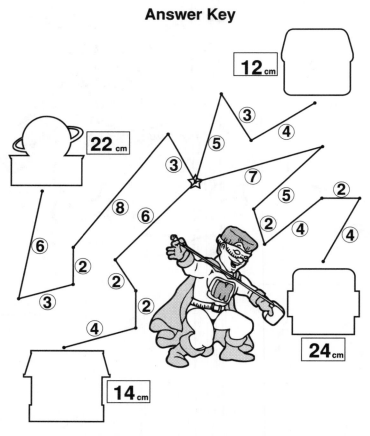

12 cm

22 cm

3

4

5

3

7

2

8

6

5

2

2

6

2

4

2

2

24 cm

3

4

14 cm

Bonus Box Answer: Answers will vary.

Name _____

A Metric Showdown

Code

1	= 1 cm
2	= 2 cm
3	= 3 cm
4	= 4 cm
5	= 5 cm
6	= 0 cm

Congratulations!

_____

Place

Congratulations!

_____

Place

To play:
1. Decorate Player 1 to look like you. Write your initial on the shirt.
2. Ask your partner to play for Metric Man (Player 2).
3. Player 1 rolls the die and draws a line from the ● that equals the distance shown in the Code.
4. Player 2 takes a turn, then Player 1, and so on.
5. Each player must draw the line length rolled. A line length may not be broken or go outside the game trail. If a line cannot be drawn, the turn is lost.
6. The first player to reach the ★ wins first place.
7. Each player labels and colors a 1st- or 2nd-place certificate.

Player 1

Player 2

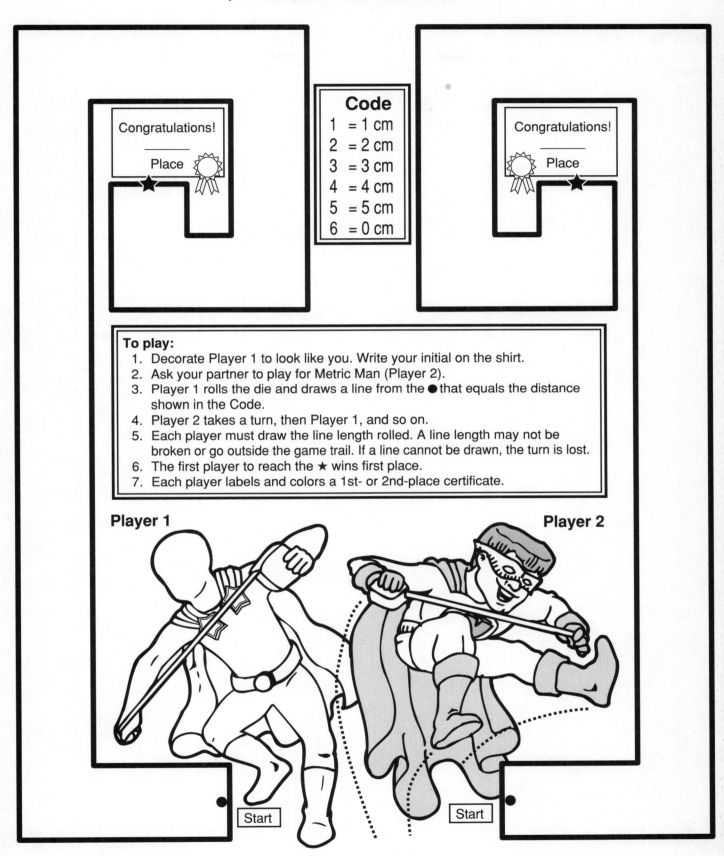

Start

Start

Materials Needed For Each Student

— pencil
— centimeter ruler
— crayons

How To Use Page 77

Provide each student with the materials listed on this page. Then pair students and give each pair one die. Have students follow the provided direcitons to play the game. •

Name _____

A Metric Masterpiece

Use a centimeter ruler.
Measure the perimeter of each shape.
Write your answers below.

Perimeter Color Code
0–11 cm = yellow
12–13 cm = red
14–16 cm = green
17–25 cm = purple

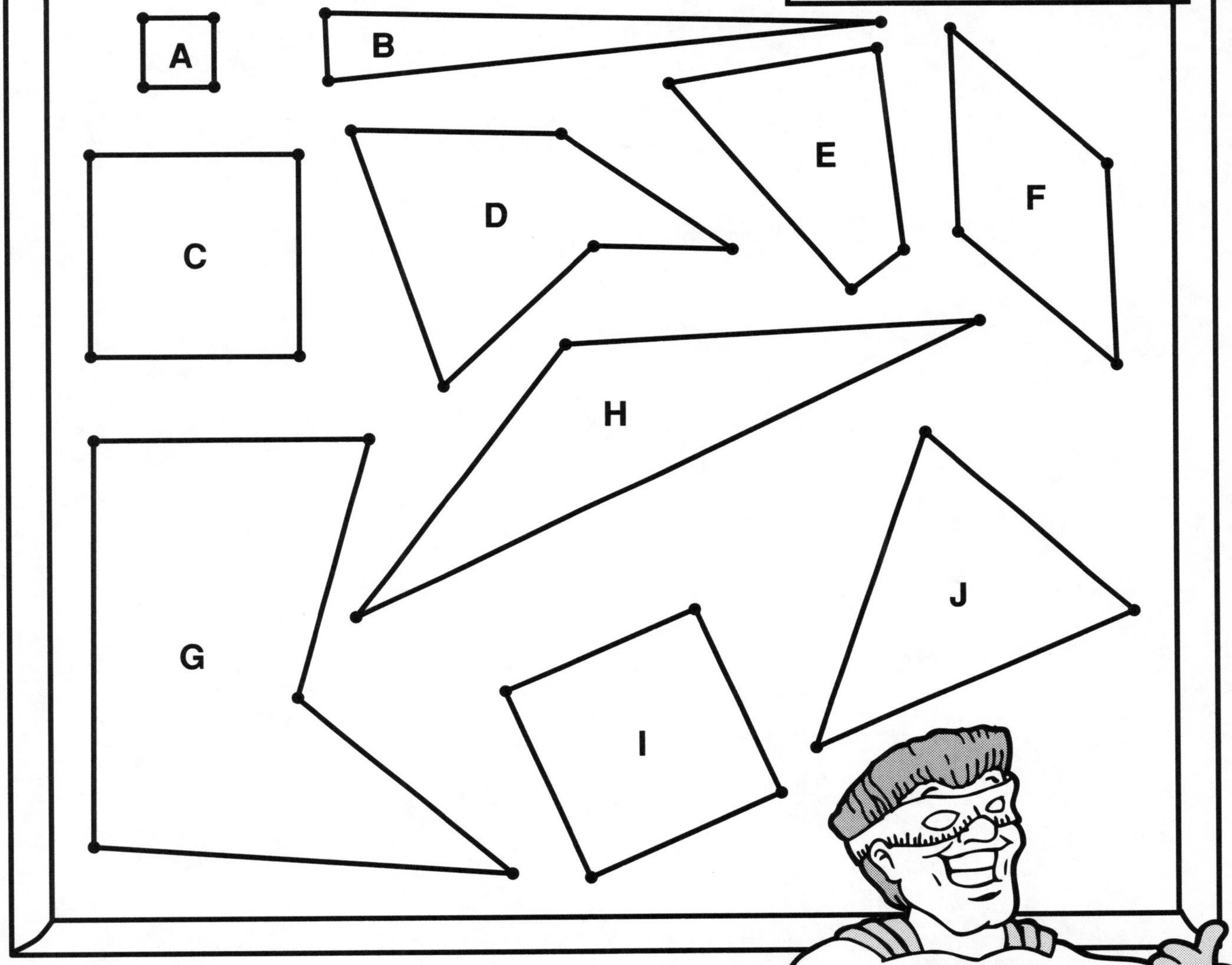

A

B

C

D

E

F

H

G

J

I

A. _____ cm

B. _____ cm

C. _____ cm

D. _____ cm

E. _____ cm

F. _____ cm

G. _____ cm

H. _____ cm

I. _____ cm

J. _____ cm

Bonus Box: Use the code to color the shapes. Color the frame brown. Color the rest of the picture blue. Well done!

Answer Key

A.   4 cm (yellow)
B. 17 cm (purple)
C. 12 cm (red)
D. 15 cm (green)
E. 11 cm (yellow)
F. 12 cm (red)
G. 24 cm (purple)
H. 21 cm (purple)
I. 12 cm (red)
J. 14 cm (green)

How Do You Measure Up?

Find each thing that is requested.
Write your answers in the stars.

Something that is 15 centimeters long.

The distance from your knee to your ankle.

The perimeter of your library book.

The length of your pencil.

The perimeter of a chalkboard eraser.

Something that is 6 centimeters long.

The height of your desk or table.

The length of a classmate's shoe.

Bonus Box: Draw a large star on the back of this paper. Inside the star write something in the classroom that you would like to measure. Measure it! Write your answer in the star.

How To Use Page 81

Review the items listed on page 81. If the items are appropriate for your classroom and students, duplicate and distribute student copies. If not, white-out the inappropriate item(s) and reprogram the corresponding star(s) as desired.

To create different versions of the scavenger hunt on page 81, photocopy the page and white-out the programming in the stars. Make this your master copy. Then program a *copy* of your master with desired items, and duplicate student copies. Using this technique, you can create a different Metric Man measurement scavenger hunt each week!

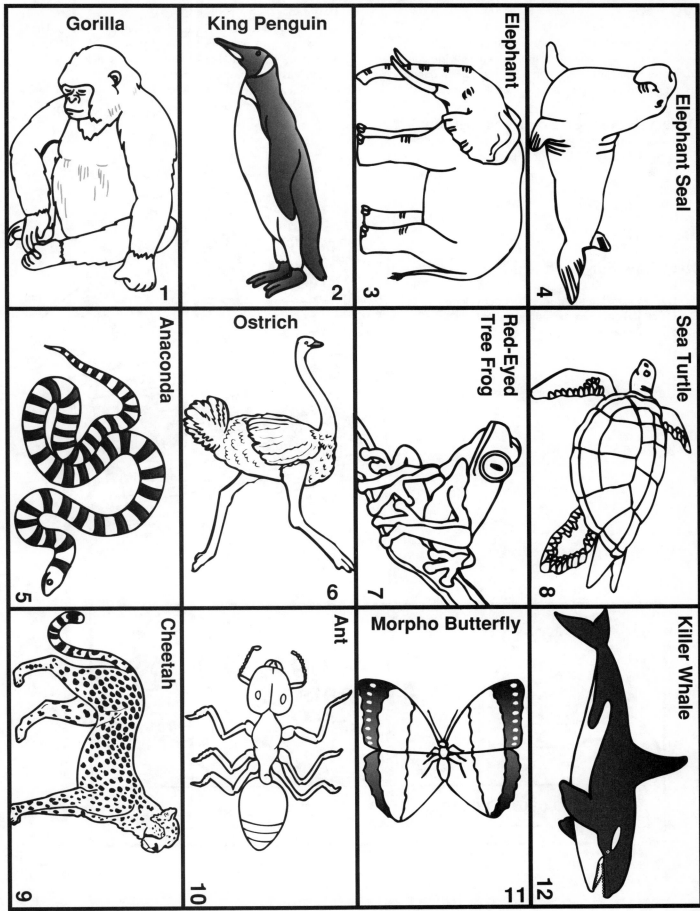

How To Use This Problem-Solving Unit
Pages 83–92

The activities in this unit are designed to give students practice using a variety of problem-solving strategies. Each student needs a set of animal cards from page 83 to complete the activities on pages 85, 89, and 91. See the directions on this page for how to make and store the animal card sets.

Materials Needed For Each Student
— white construction-paper copy of page 83
— copy of the envelope label on this page
— crayons
— pencil
— scissors
— letter-size envelope
— glue

Directions For Each Student
1. Color, personalize, and cut out the envelope label.
2. Glue the label to the front of your envelope.
3. Color and cut apart the animal cards.
4. Store the cards in the envelope.

How To Use The Animal Cards
Page 55

The animal cards can be used in a variety of ways. They are necessary to complete the problem-solving activities on pages 85, 89, and 91. The cards will also be helpful to students as they complete the activity on page 87. The extension activities on page 88 and the follow-up activity on page 90 also use the animal cards.

Assembled Project

Envelope Label

Name_____

Animals All Around

Use your animal cards to complete each diagram.

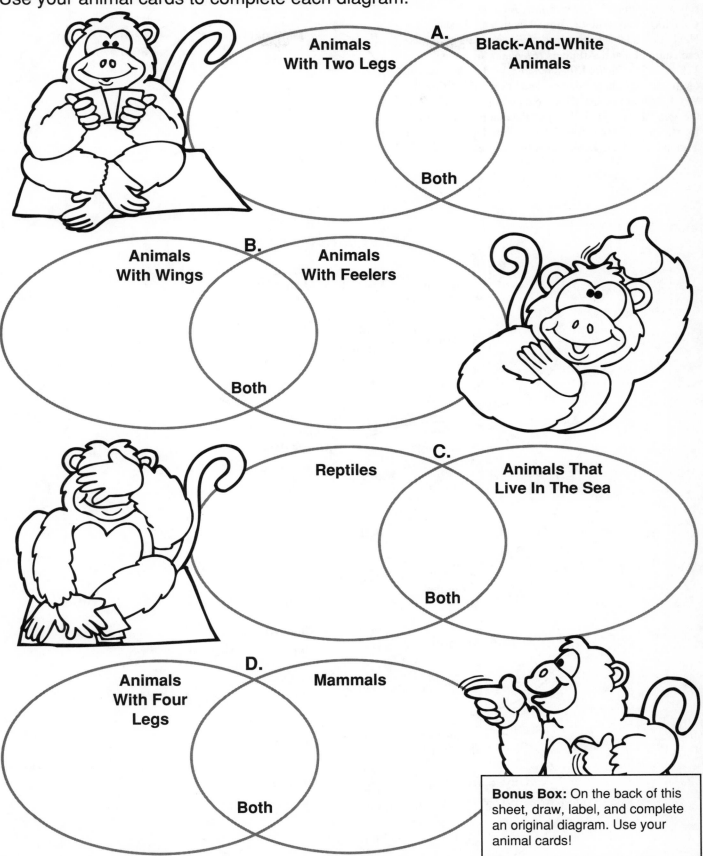

A. Animals With Two Legs — Black-And-White Animals — Both

B. Animals With Wings — Animals With Feelers — Both

C. Reptiles — Animals That Live In The Sea — Both

D. Animals With Four Legs — Mammals — Both

Bonus Box: On the back of this sheet, draw, label, and complete an original diagram. Use your animal cards!

How To Use Page 86

To introduce this activity, draw two overlapping ovals on the chalkboard and program the resulting Venn diagram as shown. Ask students to sort from their card sets each mammal *(Killer Whale, Elephant, Gorilla, Cheetah);* then write the animal names on the diagram. Next ask students to sort from their complete card sets each animal that has flippers *(Elephant Seal, King Penguin, Sea Turtle, Killer Whale)*. Write these names on the diagram, too. Lead students to see that "Killer Whale" should be listed on the diagram only once—in the area labeled "Both." Adjust the diagram and check for student understanding. Then ask students to use their animal card sets to independently complete the page.

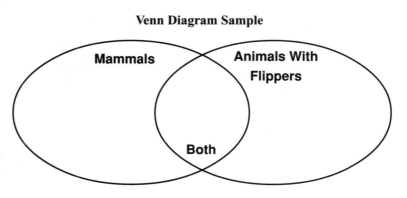

Venn Diagram Sample

Answer Key

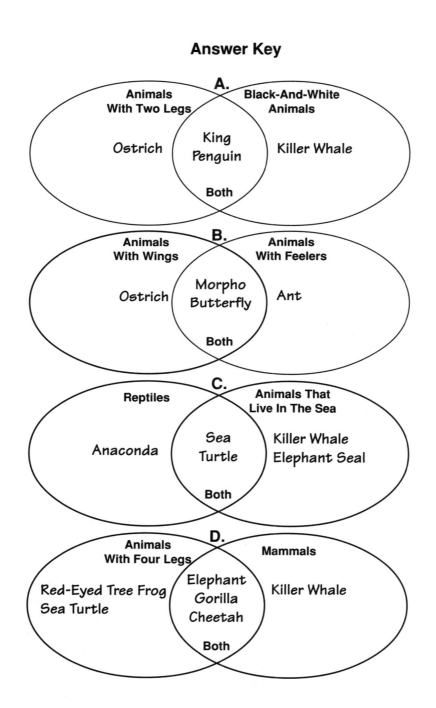

Lots Of Legs!

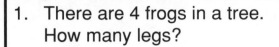

Read each problem.
Draw and color a picture of the problem in the large box.
Use your animal cards to help you.
Circle the correct answer in the small box.

1. There are 4 frogs in a tree. How many legs?	2. There are 3 elephants eating plants. How many legs?

| 12 | 16 | 18 | | 8 | 12 | 15 |

3. There are 5 ostriches and 2 butter-flies. Which group has more legs?	4. A cheetah runs by, chasing an ostrich. How many legs?

| the ostrich group | the butterfly group | | 2 | 4 | 6 |

5. There are 2 ants and 3 penguins. Which group has fewer legs?	6. How many frogs are needed to have the same number of legs as 2 ants?

| the ant group | the penguin group | | 3 | 4 | 5 |

Extension Activities

— Ask students to record on the back of each animal card any facts that they learn about the animal during your amazing animals study. Then challenge students to use the facts they have gathered to create additional problem-solving activities like "Animals All Around" on page 85 and "What Am I?" on page 89.

— This large-group problem-solving game is a cinch to make and it's easy to play. Laminate and cut out a set of the Amazing Animal cards (page 83). Store the cards in a paper bag or another small container. To play, each child needs his own set of animal cards. Ask one student to draw a laminated card from the container, concealing the illustrated animal from his classmates' view. Next the student gives one clue that could lead to the identification of the mystery animal. He then calls on a maximum of three classmates who believe they can identify the animal. If a correct answer is not given, the student states another clue about the animal and repeats the procedure. The game continues in this manner until the mystery animal is identified. The student then places the card in a discard pile. The classmate who made the correct identification begins a new round of play by selecting a card from the container.

Answer Key
1. 16
2. 12
3. the butterfly group
4. 6
5. the penguin group
6. 3

Name _____

What Am I?

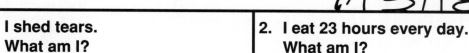

To solve each animal riddle:
Spread out your 12 animal cards.
Read the clues.
Remove each card that cannot be the secret animal.
Draw and color the secret animal in the box.

1. **I shed tears.**
   What am I?
   • I do not have flippers.
   • I do not have wings.
   • I do not have a tail.
   • I have 4 legs.
   • I am hairy.

2. **I eat 23 hours every day.**
   What am I?
   • I have a tail.
   • I do not live in or near the sea.
   • I have ears you can see.
   • I have a very big nose.

3. **I can lift 50 times my own weight.**
   What am I?
   • I have more than 2 legs.
   • I do not swim or fly.
   • I am small.
   • I do not hop.

4. **I smell with my tongue.**
   What am I?
   • I have less than 6 legs.
   • I do not have a bill.
   • I am more than one color.
   • I do not live in the sea.
   • I do not have fur.
   • I do not hop.

5. **My teeth grow my whole life.**
   What am I?
   • I do not have feelers.
   • I am not a bird.
   • I am a mammal.
   • I am very fast.
   • I live in every ocean in the world.

Bonus Box: On the back of this paper, write your own animal riddle! Find an interesting fact about one animal in your card set. Then write a set of clues.

Follow-Up Activity

Invite each child who completed the bonus box activity to trade papers with a classmate who also completed the activity. After each partner identifies his classmate's secret animal, have the two students meet to share their answers, return their partners' papers, and make adjustments to their own sets of clues as needed. Then invite each student who has tested his clues to read them aloud, in turn, for his classmates to solve.

Answer Key

(Students should draw and color each secret animal.)

1. Gorilla
2. Elephant
3. Ant
4. Anaconda
5. Killer whale

Name

Hunting For Habitats

Look at the numbers on your animal cards.
Read the clues in each habitat box.
Decide where each animal belongs.
Write the animal names on the lines.

*You'll have one animal card left over.
This tiny animal can live almost anywhere!
Write its name on the back of this paper.*

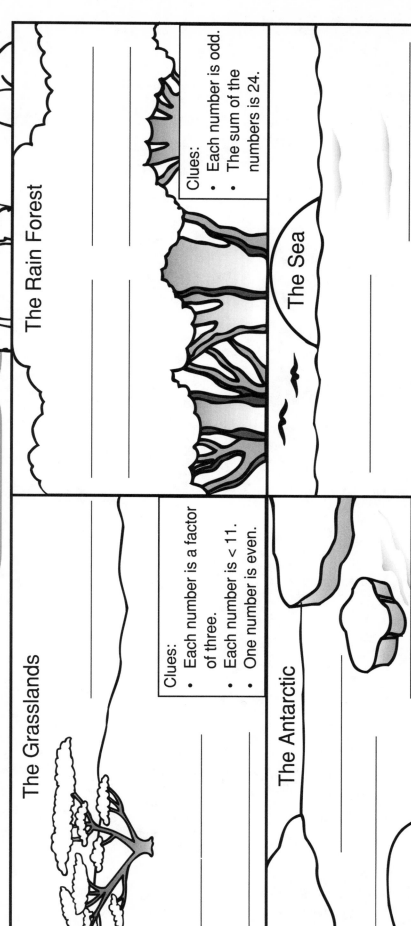

The Rain Forest

Clues:
- Each number is odd.
- The sum of the numbers is 24.

The Sea

Clues:
- Both numbers are even.
- Both numbers are > 7.
- The sum of the numbers is 20.

The Grasslands

Clues:
- Each number is a factor of three.
- Each number is < 11.
- One number is even.

The Antarctic

Clues:
- Both numbers are even.
- The numbers are < 9.
- The difference of the numbers is 2.

Answer Key

(The order of answers in each habitat will vary.)

The Grasslands
Cheetah
Elephant
Ostrich

The Rain Forest
Anaconda
Red-Eyed Tree Frog
Morpho Butterfly
Gorilla

The Antarctic
King Penguin
Elephant Seal

The Sea
Killer Whale
Sea Turtle

("Ant" should be written on the back of each child's paper.)

A Very Confused Camper!

Bub Cub has lost the first page of his daily camp schedule.
Carefully read the notes he's taken.
On the lines, write a new schedule for Bub.

Things To Remember
- ✔ After the hike, go to the picnic area for a snack.
- ✔ Be at the dining hall by 7:30 for breakfast.
- ✔ When you hear Bear Call, get out of bed!
- ✔ After breakfast always brush your teeth.
- ✔ Lunch is at 12:00.
- ✔ When you finish your snack, it's time for arts and crafts.
- ✔ Swimming lessons are right before lunch.
- ✔ Make your bed before breakfast.
- ✔ At 8:30 meet at the big tree for a nature hike.

A New Schedule For Bub Cub

- • _____
- • _____
- • _____
- • _____
- • _____
- • _____
- • _____
- • _____
- • _____

Bonus Box: On the back of this page, list five things that you think Bub Cub might do after lunch. Write the events in the order that they would occur.

How To Use This Problem-Solving Unit
Pages 93–100

The activities in this unit are designed to give students practice in using a variety of problem-solving strategies. For best results discuss each student page as it is presented. If desired, work a portion of each activity as a class before students work independently.

Answer Key

When you hear Bear Call, get out of bed!
Make your bed before breakfast.
Be at the dining hall by 7:30 for breakfast.
After breakfast always brush your teeth.
At 8:30 meet at the big tree for a nature hike.
After the hike, go to the picnic area for a snack.
When you finish your snack, it's time for arts and crafts.
Swimming lessons are right before lunch.
Lunch is at 12:00.

Name _____

The Hug-A-Cub Cookout

Saturday is the camp cookout.
Happy Trails Cabin must complete its food order.

There are 8 bear cubs in Happy Trails Cabin.
Finish each chart to find out how much food to order.

Each cub will eat 2 hot dogs.

Number of bear cubs	0	1	2	3	4	5	6	7	8
Number of hot dogs	0	2	4	6					

Sweet Pickles

Each cub will eat 5 pickles.

Number of bear cubs	0	1	2	3	4	5	6	7	8
Number of pickles	0	5	10	15					

Each cub will eat 8 potato chips.

Number of bear cubs	0	1	2	3	4	5	6	7	8
Number of potato chips	0	8	16						

Potato Chips
Cub Size

Each cub will eat 4 cookies.

Number of bear cubs	0	1	2	3	4	5	6	7	8
Number of cookies	0	4	8						

Each cub will eat 3 marshmallows.

Number of bear cubs	0	1	2	3	4	5	6	7	8
Number of marshmallows	0	3	6						

Bear-In-Mind
Marshmallows

Use the completed charts to fill out the food order form.

Camp Cookout Food Order

Cabin: _____

Number of each:

_____ hot dogs   _____ potato chips
_____ pickles   _____ cookies   _____ marshmallows

Answer Key

Each cub will eat 2 hot dogs.

Number of bear cubs	0	1	2	3	4	5	6	7	8
Number of hot dogs	0	2	4	6	**8**	**10**	**12**	**14**	**16**

Each cub will eat 5 pickles.

Number of bear cubs	0	1	2	3	4	5	6	7	8
Number of pickles	0	5	10	15	**20**	**25**	**30**	**35**	**40**

Each cub will eat 8 potato chips.

Number of bear cubs	0	1	2	3	4	5	6	7	8
Number of potato chips	0	8	16	**24**	**32**	**40**	**48**	**56**	**64**

Each cub will eat 4 cookies.

Number of bear cubs	0	1	2	3	4	5	6	7	8
Number of cookies	0	4	8	**12**	**16**	**20**	**24**	**28**	**32**

Each cub will eat 3 marshmallows.

Number of bear cubs	0	1	2	3	4	5	6	7	8
Number of marshmallows	0	3	6	**9**	**12**	**15**	**18**	**21**	**24**

Camp Cookout Food Order

Cabin: *Happy Trails*

Number of each:

16 hot dogs	**64** potato chips		
40 pickles	**32** cookies	**24** marshmallows	

A Cub Sing-Along

Each night the bear cubs sing around the campfire.
Bub Cub is confused! What does he wear? Where does he sit?

Color each cub's T-shirt.
Use these clues.

- Four of the cubs wear purple Camp Hug-a-Cub T-shirts.
- Four of the cubs wear yellow Camp Hug-a-Cub T-shirts.
- Bonnie is wearing her purple T-shirt.
- Betsy is wearing her yellow T-shirt.
- B. C. and Bert are dressed like Bonnie.
- Barney is dressed like Betsy.
- Brian and Becca wear the same color of T-shirt.

Bub wears his _____ T-shirt.

Cut on the dotted lines.
Glue the bears around the campfire.
Use these clues.

- Betsy Bear sits across the campfire from Barney.
- Bert sits in between Betsy and Brian.
- Becca sits across from Brian and next to Bonnie.
- B. C. sits next to Barney.

Bub sits between _____ and _____.

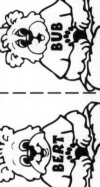

BUB · BERT · BRIAN · BECCA · B. C. · BETSY

BARNEY

BONNIE

97

Answer Key
Bub wears his **purple** T-shirt.
Bub sits between **Betsy** and **Becca.**

Barney
yellow

Bonnie
purple

B. C.
purple

Becca
yellow

X

Brian
yellow

Bub
purple

Bert
purple

Betsy
yellow

Name _____

Gifts From Camp

Buzzy Bear has $10.00 to spend on camp souvenirs.
He is buying a backpack for himself and a stuffed bee for his sister.
Show five different ways that Buzzy can spend all of his money.

Souvenirs

backpack	$ 5.00
stuffed bee	$ 3.00
cub cap	$ 2.00
sunglasses	$ 1.00
key ring	$ .75
bookmark	$ .75
pencil	$ .50
postcard	$ .25

Spending Plan #1

How Many?	Item	Unit Price	Total
1	backpack	5.00	5.00
1	stuffed bee	3.00	3.00
	Total Spent		$

Spending Plan #2

How Many?	Item	Unit Price	Total
	Total Spent		$

Spending Plan #3

How Many?	Item	Unit Price	Total
	Total Spent		$

Spending Plan #4

How Many?	Item	Unit Price	Total
	Total Spent		$

Spending Plan #5

How Many?	Item	Unit Price	Total
	Total Spent		$

Answer Key
(Answers will vary; however, each plan should equal $10.00 and include a backpack and a stuffed bee.)

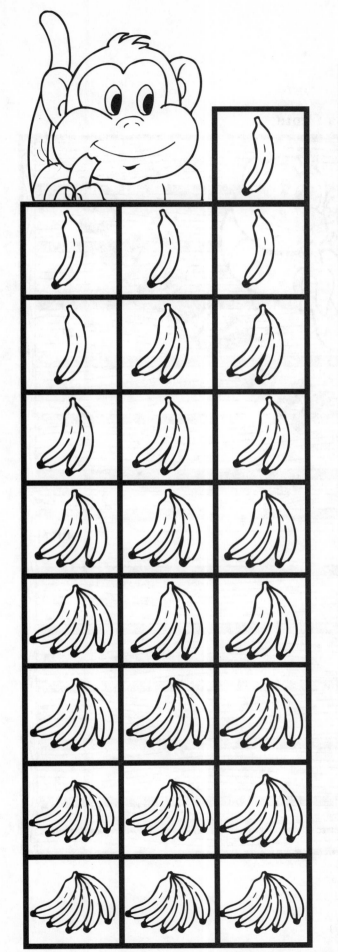

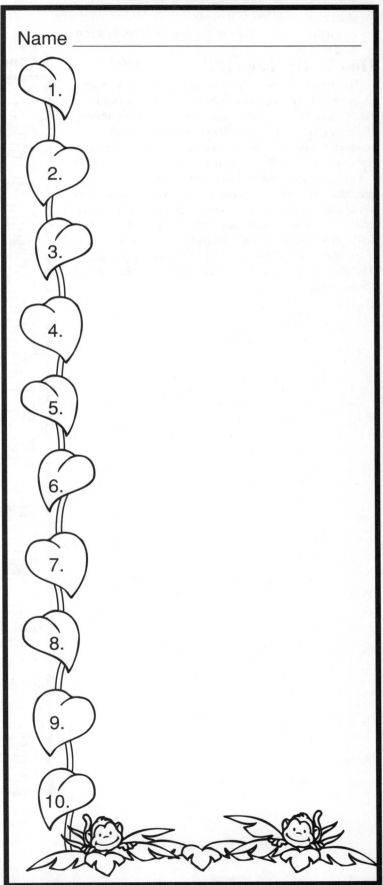

Name _____

1.

2.

3.

4.

5.

6.

7.

8.

9.

10.

Materials Needed For Each Student
— crayons
— scissors
— glue, tape, or access to a stapler
— construction-paper copy of the banana crate on this page

How To Use Page 101

Have each student color and cut out the banana cards on page 101. Dictate a multiplication fact with factors of five or less. Have students write the fact on their answer sheets and use their manipulatives to determine the product. Continue in this manner until ten different facts have been solved. Or program a copy of the activity with ten multiplication facts; then make student copies of the programmed activity. Another alternative is to have each student create and solve ten problems on his own. At the end of the activity, have each student color, cut out, and fold a construction paper copy of the banana crate; then glue, tape, or staple the sides closed to form a pocket. The students can store their manipulatives in these crates for later use.

Banana Crate

Fold back.

Name

Name _____

Going Bananas!

Solve each problem.
Color the bananas yellow as you use the answers.

5 x 4	3 x 2	2 x 2	2 x 9	8 x 1
4 x 7	5 x 2	3 x 5	4 x 8	2 x 6
2 x 3	4 x 2	3 x 4	2 x 5	4 x 1

5 x 1	2 x 8	5 x 3	3 x 3	5 x 6	3 x 9
3 x 8	5 x 5	4 x 9	2 x 4	5 x 8	5 x 9
5 x 7	4 x 6	9 x 1	4 x 0	4 x 3	

2 x 7 = _____   6 x 3 = _____   4 x 4 = _____

4 x 5 = _____   5 x 0 = _____   3 x 7 = _____

Answer Key

5 x 4 **20**	3 x 2 **6**	2 x 2 **4**	2 x 9 **18**	8 x 1 **8**
4 x 7 **28**	5 x 2 **10**	3 x 5 **15**	4 x 8 **32**	2 x 6 **12**
2 x 3 **6**	4 x 2 **8**	3 x 4 **12**	2 x 5 **10**	4 x 1 **4**

5 x 1 **5**	2 x 8 **16**	5 x 3 **15**	3 x 3 **9**	5 x 6 **30**	3 x 9 **27**
3 x 8 **24**	5 x 5 **25**	4 x 9 **36**	2 x 4 **8**	5 x 8 **40**	5 x 9 **45**

5 x 7 **35**	4 x 6 **24**	9 x 1 **9**	4 x 0 **0**	4 x 3 **12**

2 x 7 = __14__   6 x 3 = __18__   4 x 4 = __16__

4 x 5 = __20__   5 x 0 = __0__   3 x 7 = __21__

Name _____

Monkey See, Monkey Do

Solve each problem.

If the answer is **even**, draw an **O** on the square.

If the answer is **odd**, draw an **X** on the square.

Game A

5 x 6	9 x 4	3 x 5
9 x 3	2 x 8	5 x 7
8 x 5	9 x 9	6 x 7

Game D

5 x 4	9 x 6	7 x 3
6 x 6	3 x 1	4 x 7
7 x 7	5 x 5	8 x 7

Game B

6 x 3	5 x 9	8 x 8
9 x 1	3 x 7	2 x 5
7 x 6	9 x 7	3 x 3

Game C

2 x 7	8 x 4	6 x 8
1 x 5	7 x 9	4 x 6
7 x 5	9 x 8	9 x 5

Write X or O to show who won each game!

Game Winners

Game A _____

Game B _____

Game C _____

Game D _____

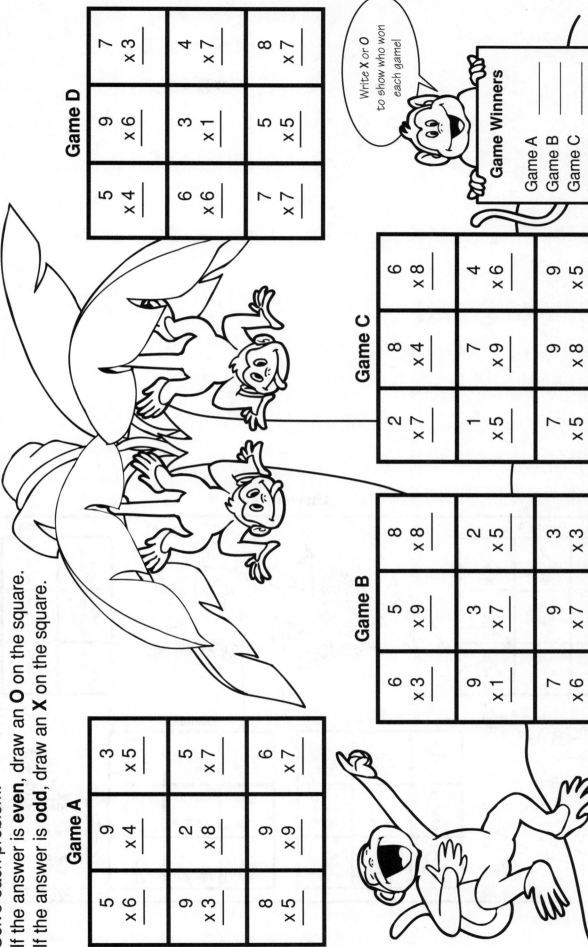

Answer Key

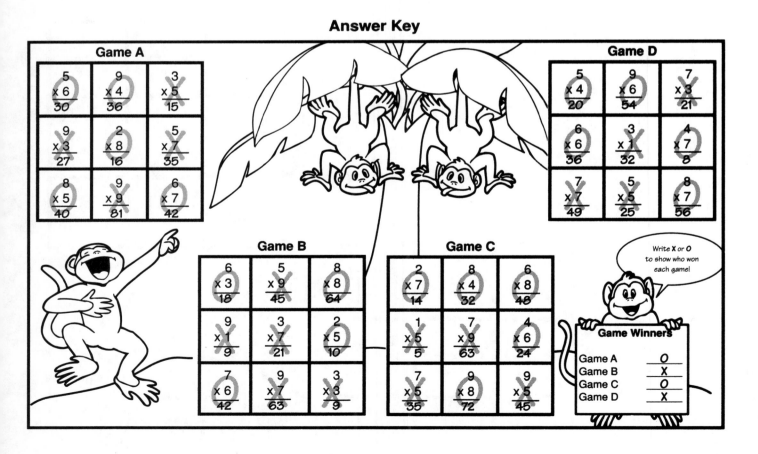

Game A

5 x 6 = 30	9 x 4 = 36	3 x 5 = 15
9 x 3 = 27	2 x 8 = 16	5 x 7 = 35
8 x 5 = 40	9 x 9 = 81	6 x 7 = 42

Game D

5 x 4 = 20	9 x 6 = 54	7 x 3 = 21
6 x 6 = 36	3 x 1 = 32	4 x 7 = 8
7 x 7 = 49	5 x 5 = 25	8 x 7 = 56

Game B

6 x 3 = 18	5 x 9 = 45	8 x 8 = 64
9 x 1 = 9	3 x 7 = 21	2 x 5 = 10
7 x 6 = 42	9 x 7 = 63	3 x 3 = 9

Game C

2 x 7 = 14	8 x 4 = 32	6 x 8 = 48
1 x 5 = 5	7 x 9 = 63	4 x 6 = 24
7 x 5 = 35	9 x 8 = 72	9 x 5 = 45

Write X or O to show who won each game!

Game Winners

Game A	O
Game B	X
Game C	O
Game D	X

Name_____

New Tire Needed

Fanny Flamingo needs your help!
Multiply each number on the tire by the center number.
One answer is done for you.

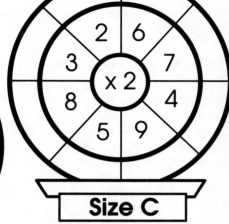

Size C

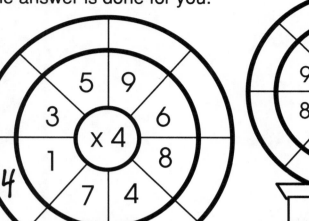

Size A

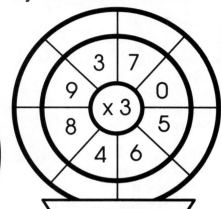

Size B

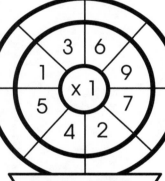

Size D

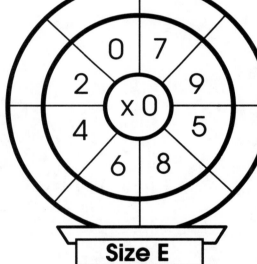

Size E

Find the tire that has the same answers as Fanny's flat.
Color this tire pink!

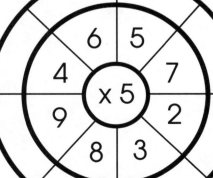

Size F

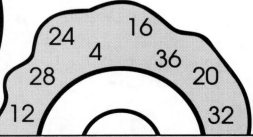

Bonus Box: On the back of this paper, draw and color the car you think Fanny Flamingo drives.

How To Use This Multiplication Unit
Pages 107–118

Tune up your youngsters' multiplication facts with this fine-feathered collection of easy-to-use reproducibles! See the back of each skill sheet for one or more ways to extend the use of the activity.

Suggestions For Reprogramming
Page 107

For additional practice with factors zero through five, make a copy of the page. White-out the number in the center of each tire. Use the same set of numbers (0–5) to reprogram the page, featuring each number on a new tire. Then duplicate the activity and create a corresponding answer key.

To increase the difficulty of the activity, make a copy of the page. White-out the number in the center of each tire and the numbers on the flat tire at the bottom of the page. Reprogram the center of each tire with a desired factor. Reprogram the flat tire with answers that correspond to one tire on the page. Then duplicate the activity and create a corresponding answer key.

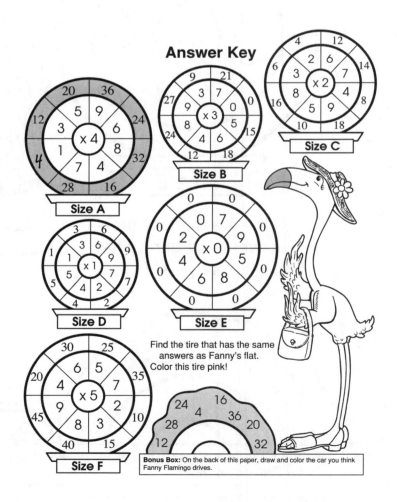

Answer Key

Find the tire that has the same answers as Fanny's flat. Color this tire pink!

Bonus Box: On the back of this paper, draw and color the car you think Fanny Flamingo drives.

Name_____

Lift And Look

For each letter,
write a problem that equals the answer on the pole.
Each problem must be a factor of 6 or 7.
Solve the problem.

a. ☐
×☐
___

b. ☐
×☐
___

c. ☐
×☐
___

d. ☐
×☐
___

e. ☐
×☐
___

f. ☐
×☐
___

g. ☐
×☐
___

h. ☐
×☐
___

i. ☐
×☐
___

j. ☐
×☐
___

k. ☐
×☐
___

l. ☐
×☐
___

m. ☐
×☐
___

n. ☐
×☐
___

o. ☐
×☐
___

p. ☐
×☐
___

q. ☐
×☐
___

r. ☐
×☐
___

s. ☐
×☐
___

t. ☐
×☐
___

a.	14
b.	18
c.	28
d.	54
e.	49
f.	36
g.	21
h.	0
i.	6
j.	42
k.	48
l.	56
m.	35
n.	12
o.	30
p.	63
q.	7
r.	24
s.	0
t.	42

Bonus Box: On the back of this paper, write the number 12. Then write six different multiplication problems that equal 12.

Suggestions For Reprogramming
Page 109

For a less challenging activity, make a copy of the page. White-out the products shown on the pole, leaving the letters intact. Choose two factors that are less than six, and reprogram the pole with products of each factor. Reprogram the Bonus Box if desired. Then duplicate the activity and create a corresponding answer key.

For a more challenging activity, make a copy of the page. White-out the products shown on the pole, leaving the letters intact. Choose two factors that are greater than seven, and reprogram the pole with products of each factor. Reprogram the Bonus Box if desired. Then duplicate the activity and create a corresponding answer key.

Answer Key

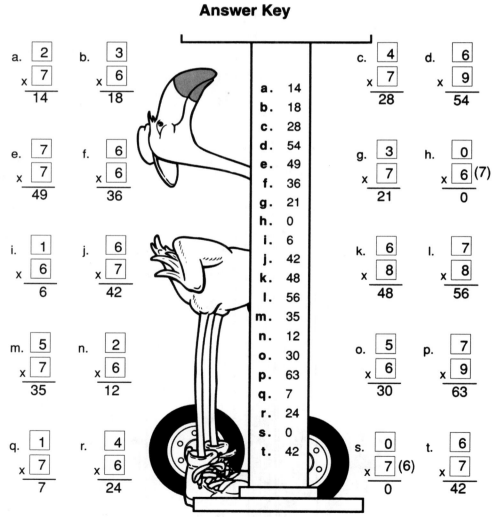

a. $\begin{array}{r} 2 \\ \times\ 7 \\ \hline 14 \end{array}$ b. $\begin{array}{r} 3 \\ \times\ 6 \\ \hline 18 \end{array}$

e. $\begin{array}{r} 7 \\ \times\ 7 \\ \hline 49 \end{array}$ f. $\begin{array}{r} 6 \\ \times\ 6 \\ \hline 36 \end{array}$

i. $\begin{array}{r} 1 \\ \times\ 6 \\ \hline 6 \end{array}$ j. $\begin{array}{r} 6 \\ \times\ 7 \\ \hline 42 \end{array}$

m. $\begin{array}{r} 5 \\ \times\ 7 \\ \hline 35 \end{array}$ n. $\begin{array}{r} 2 \\ \times\ 6 \\ \hline 12 \end{array}$

q. $\begin{array}{r} 1 \\ \times\ 7 \\ \hline 7 \end{array}$ r. $\begin{array}{r} 4 \\ \times\ 6 \\ \hline 24 \end{array}$

a.	14
b.	18
c.	28
d.	54
e.	49
f.	36
g.	21
h.	0
i.	6
j.	42
k.	48
l.	56
m.	35
n.	12
o.	30
p.	63
q.	7
r.	24
s.	0
t.	42

c. $\begin{array}{r} 4 \\ \times\ 7 \\ \hline 28 \end{array}$ d. $\begin{array}{r} 6 \\ \times\ 9 \\ \hline 54 \end{array}$

g. $\begin{array}{r} 3 \\ \times\ 7 \\ \hline 21 \end{array}$ h. $\begin{array}{r} 0 \\ \times\ 6\ (7) \\ \hline 0 \end{array}$

k. $\begin{array}{r} 6 \\ \times\ 8 \\ \hline 48 \end{array}$ l. $\begin{array}{r} 7 \\ \times\ 8 \\ \hline 56 \end{array}$

o. $\begin{array}{r} 5 \\ \times\ 6 \\ \hline 30 \end{array}$ p. $\begin{array}{r} 7 \\ \times\ 9 \\ \hline 63 \end{array}$

s. $\begin{array}{r} 0 \\ \times\ 7\ (6) \\ \hline 0 \end{array}$ t. $\begin{array}{r} 6 \\ \times\ 7 \\ \hline 42 \end{array}$

Bonus Box Answer: 12 *(The order of these facts will vary.)*

$12 \times 1 = 12$	$4 \times 3 = 12$	$6 \times 2 = 12$
$1 \times 12 = 12$	$3 \times 4 = 12$	$2 \times 6 = 12$

Name_____

Ready To Repair

Use the code.
Write each missing factor.
Solve each problem.

Flamingo Service

Flamingo Auto Repair

Code: △ = 7   ○ = 8   □ = 9

a. △ x 7 = _____   9 x □ = _____   □ x 4 = _____

b.
```
  2        △        3        ○        6        □        ○
x ○      x 8      x □      x 9      x △      x 8      x 5
___      ___      ___      ___      ___      ___      ___
```

c. 2 x □ = _____   7 x ○ = _____   ○ x 4 = _____

d.
```
  △        5        □        ○        △        ○        5
x 4      x △      x 7      x 1      x 2      x 8      x □
___      ___      ___      ___      ___      ___      ___
```

e. □ x 6 = _____   7 x △ = _____   9 x ○ = _____

f.
```
  1        ○        5        3        □        5        △
x △      x 6      x □      x △      x 1      x ○      x 9
___      ___      ___      ___      ___      ___      ___
```

Suggestions For Reprogramming
Page 111

For a less challenging activity, make a copy of the page. White-out one or more factors shown in the code. Replace each missing factor with a desired number. Then duplicate the activity and create a corresponding answer key.

For additional practice with factors seven, eight, and nine, make a copy of the page. White-out the factors shown in the code. Use the same factors (7, 8, 9) to reprogram the code, pairing each number with a new shape. Then duplicate the activity and create a corresponding answer key.

For a more challenging activity, make a copy of the page. White-out one or more factors shown in the code. Replace each missing factor with a desired number. Then duplicate the activity and create a corresponding answer key.

Answer Key

Code: △ = 7   ◯ = 8   ▢ = 9

a. △ x 7 = __49__   9 x ▢ = __81__   ▢ x 4 = __36__

b.
$$\begin{array}{ccccccc} 2 & △ & 3 & ⑧ & 6 & ▣ & ⑧ \\ \times ⑧ & \times 8 & \times ▣ & \times 9 & \times △ & \times 8 & \times 5 \\ \hline 16 & 56 & 27 & 72 & 42 & 72 & 40 \end{array}$$

c. 2 x ▢ = __18__   7 x ⑧ = __56__   ⑧ x 4 = __32__

d.
$$\begin{array}{ccccccc} △ & 5 & ▣ & ⑧ & △ & ⑧ & 5 \\ \times 4 & \times △ & \times 7 & \times 1 & \times 2 & \times 8 & \times ▣ \\ \hline 28 & 35 & 63 & 8 & 14 & 64 & 45 \end{array}$$

e. ▢ x 6 = __54__   7 x △ = __49__   9 x ⑧ = __72__

f.
$$\begin{array}{ccccccc} 1 & ⑧ & 5 & 3 & ▣ & 5 & △ \\ \times △ & \times 6 & \times ▣ & \times △ & \times 1 & \times ⑧ & \times 9 \\ \hline 7 & 48 & 45 & 21 & 9 & 40 & 63 \end{array}$$

112

Name_____

Road Test

Solve the problems.

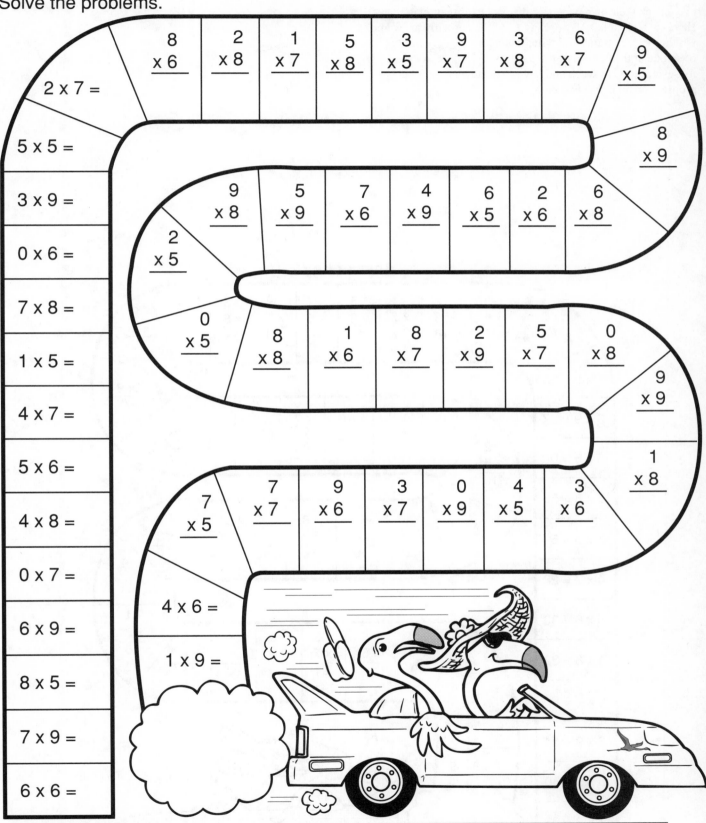

| 8 x 6 | 2 x 8 | 1 x 7 | 5 x 8 | 3 x 5 | 9 x 7 | 3 x 8 | 6 x 7 |
| 9 x 5 |
| 8 x 9 |

2 x 7 =

5 x 5 =

3 x 9 =

0 x 6 =

7 x 8 =

1 x 5 =

4 x 7 =

5 x 6 =

4 x 8 =

0 x 7 =

6 x 9 =

8 x 5 =

7 x 9 =

6 x 6 =

| 9 x 8 | 5 x 9 | 7 x 6 | 4 x 9 | 6 x 5 | 2 x 6 | 6 x 8 |

2 x 5

0 x 5

| 8 x 8 | 1 x 6 | 8 x 7 | 2 x 9 | 5 x 7 | 0 x 8 |

9 x 9

1 x 8

| 7 x 5 | 7 x 7 | 9 x 6 | 3 x 7 | 0 x 9 | 4 x 5 | 3 x 6 |

4 x 6 =

1 x 9 =

Bonus Box: Pretend you are riding along with Fanny Flamingo. On the back of this paper, write where you would ask her to take you and why. Then draw and color a picture of the place. Vroom!

How To Extend The Use Of Page 113

To use the activity as a speed drill, challenge each child to answer as many of the 50 facts as she can within an allotted time frame. Then read aloud the correct answers so students may check their own papers or the papers of their classmates. Have each child tally how many facts she correctly answered within the time frame and write this number in the empty puff of smoke at the bottom of the page. If desired, repeat the activity several times a week and have each student chart her progress on an individual bar graph.

Answer Key

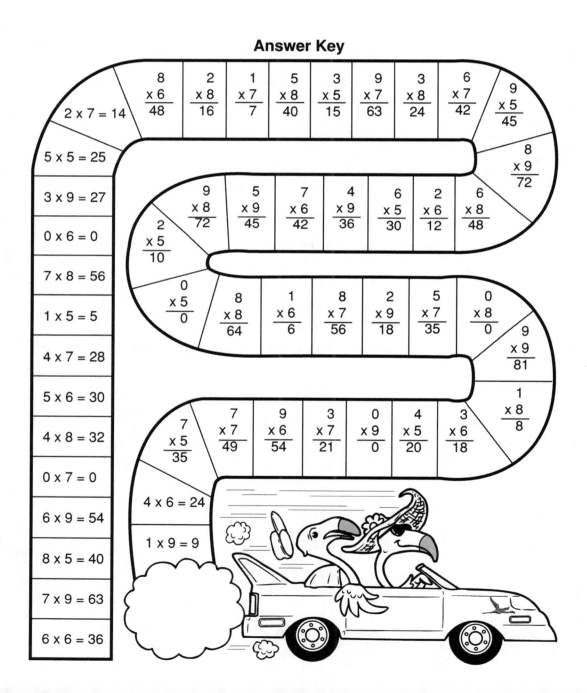

Name _____

Another Look Under The Hood

Thank you so much!

One more quart of Bird state Oil and you will be on your way!

1BIGBIRD

Code

6	7	8
3	4	1
9	5	2

Use the code.
Write a number in each shape; then multiply.
One problem is done for you.

1. $\boxed{9}$ x $\boxed{3}$ = 27

2. $\square$ x $\square$ = $\square$

3. $\square$ x $\square$ = $\square$

4. $\square$ x $\square$ = $\square$

5. $\square$ x $\square$ = $\square$

6. $\square$ x $\square$ = $\square$

7. $\square$ x $\square$ = $\square$

8. $\square$ x $\square$ = $\square$

9. $\square$ x $\square$ = $\square$

10. $\square$ x $\square$ = $\square$

11. $\boxed{}$ x $\square$ = $\square$

12. $\square$ x $\square$ = $\square$

13. $\square$ x $\square$ = $\square$

14. $\square$ x $\square$ = $\square$

15. $\square$ x $\square$ = $\square$

16. $\square$ x $\square$ = $\square$

17. $\square$ x $\square$ = $\square$

18. $\square$ x $\square$ = $\square$

19. $\square$ x $\square$ = $\square$

20. $\square$ x $\square$ = $\square$

Bonus Box: On the back of this sheet, write a new code for the numbers one through nine. Use the code to write five multiplication problems. Ask a classmate to solve the problems. Then check your classmate's work.

Suggestions For Reprogramming
Page 115

For additional practice with factors one through nine, make a copy of the page. White-out the numbers in the code. Use the same set of numbers (1–9) to reprogram the code, featuring each number in a new location. Then duplicate the activity and create a corresponding answer key.

To adjust the difficulty of the page, make a copy of the activity. White-out the numbers in the code. Use a desired set of numbers from 0 to 12 to reprogram the code. Reprogram the Bonus Box as needed. Then duplicate the activity and create a corresponding answer key.

Answer Key

1. $9 \times 3 = 27$
2. $6 \times 2 = 12$
3. $5 \times 5 = 25$
4. $1 \times 8 = 8$
5. $7 \times 9 = 63$
6. $6 \times 6 = 36$
7. $1 \times 7 = 7$
8. $9 \times 9 = 81$
9. $2 \times 4 = 8$
10. $8 \times 5 = 40$

11. $2 \times 9 = 18$
12. $4 \times 4 = 16$
13. $3 \times 3 = 9$
14. $4 \times 7 = 28$
15. $8 \times 9 = 72$
16. $5 \times 1 = 5$
17. $4 \times 8 = 32$
18. $7 \times 4 = 28$
19. $3 \times 6 = 18$
20. $8 \times 2 = 16$

Name_____

Fill 'er Up!

It has been a very busy day at Flamingo Fuel & Auto Repair!
Find the total of each gas ticket.
Use the prices on the gas pump.

A. Best Gas
   Three gallons

B. Cheap Gas
   Five gallons

C. Cheap Gas
   Eight gallons

D. Good Gas
   Six gallons

E. Best Gas
   Ten gallons

F. Cheap Gas
   Four gallons

G. Good Gas
   Nine gallons

H. Cheap Gas
   Twelve gallons

I. Best Gas
   Seven gallons

J. Good Gas
   Eleven gallons

K. Good Gas
   Two gallons

L. Best Gas
   Five gallons

Gas Pump

**Flamingo
Fuel**

$00.00

Best Gas	=	12¢ per gallon
Good Gas	=	11¢ per gallon
Cheap Gas	=	10¢ per gallon

Bonus Box: Color each ticket.
   Pink   =   total is more than 75¢
   Yellow =   total is less than 75¢

Suggestions For Reprogramming
Page 117

For a less challenging activity, make a copy of the page. White-out the gas prices shown on the gas pump and replace them with three desired factors, making sure the Best Gas has the highest price and the Cheap Gas has the lowest. Reprogram the money amounts listed in the Bonus Box in a similar manner. Then duplicate the activity and create a corresponding answer key.

Answer Key

A. 36¢
B. 50¢
C. 80¢
D. 66¢
E. 120¢ or $1.20
F. 40¢
G. 99¢
H. 120¢ or $1.20
I. 84¢
J. 121¢ or $1.21
K. 22¢
L. 60¢

Bonus Box Answer:

Color of Tickets
A. yellow
B. yellow
C. pink
D. yellow
E. pink
F. yellow
G. pink
H. pink
I. pink
J. pink
K. yellow
L. yellow

Name _____

Cookie Capers

Cut out the cookies.
Use all 16 cookies to complete the chart.

Total Cookies	People Sharing	Cookies Per Person	Leftover Cookies
	3		
	4		
	5		
	6		
	8		

Use a different number of cookies to complete this chart.
You must use at least 8 cookies.

Total Cookies	People Sharing	Cookies Per Person	Leftover Cookies
	2		
	3		
	5		
	7		
	8		

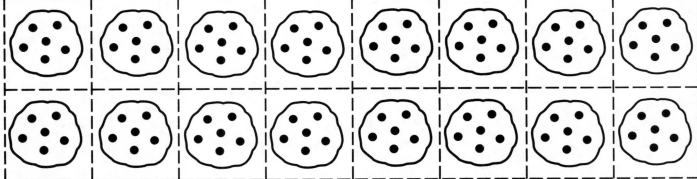

How To Use Page 119

Have students cut out the cookies at the bottom of the page; then, as a group, complete the first row of the top chart. To do this have each student fill in the total number of cookies (16) and determine how many people will be sharing the cookies (3). Instruct each student to divide his 16 cookie cutouts into three equal groups—setting aside any leftover cookies. Next have each student fill in the number of cookies each person would get (5) and the number of leftover cookies (1). Students can complete the rest of the chart individually, using all 16 cookies each time. Students complete the second chart on their own.

If desired, duplicate extra copies of page 119 so that students can complete additional charts using a different number of cookies for each chart. To investigate numbers greater than 16, have two or more children combine their cookie cutouts.

Answer Key

Chart #1

Total Cookies	People Sharing	Cookies Per Person	Leftover Cookies
16	3	5	1
16	4	4	0
16	5	3	1
16	6	2	4
16	8	2	0

Chart #2
Answers will vary.

Name_____

Gathering Cookie Clues

Divide the cookies and draw them in the jars.
Write the number of cookies in each jar on its lid.
Write the division equation that describes what you did.

Under Official Investigation

Investigator Crumb

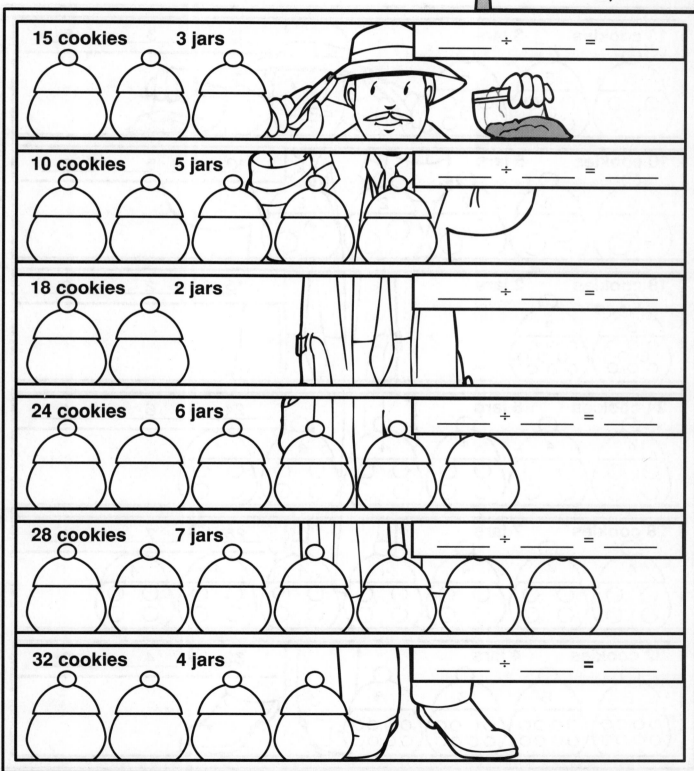

15 cookies   **3 jars**   ____ ÷ ____ = ____

10 cookies   **5 jars**   ____ ÷ ____ = ____

18 cookies   **2 jars**   ____ ÷ ____ = ____

24 cookies   **6 jars**   ____ ÷ ____ = ____

28 cookies   **7 jars**   ____ ÷ ____ = ____

32 cookies   **4 jars**   ____ ÷ ____ = ____

Answer Key

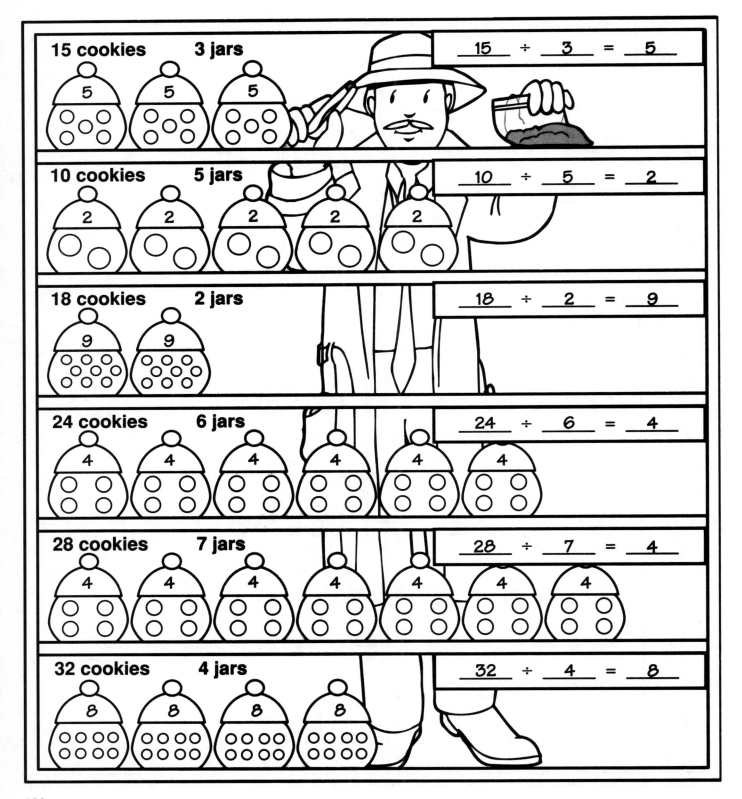

15 cookies   3 jars   15 ÷ 3 = 5

10 cookies   5 jars   10 ÷ 5 = 2

18 cookies   2 jars   18 ÷ 2 = 9

24 cookies   6 jars   24 ÷ 6 = 4

28 cookies   7 jars   28 ÷ 7 = 4

32 cookies   4 jars   32 ÷ 4 = 8

Name _____

A Colossal Cookie!

Find out if Investigator Crumb has solved the cookie case.

🍪 Solve each problem.

🍪 Check off each answer on the investigator's list.

🍪 Add the chocolate chips. Use the secret code.

🍪 Count the chocolate chips you've added.

🍪 Compare your total to the total at the bottom of the investigator's list.

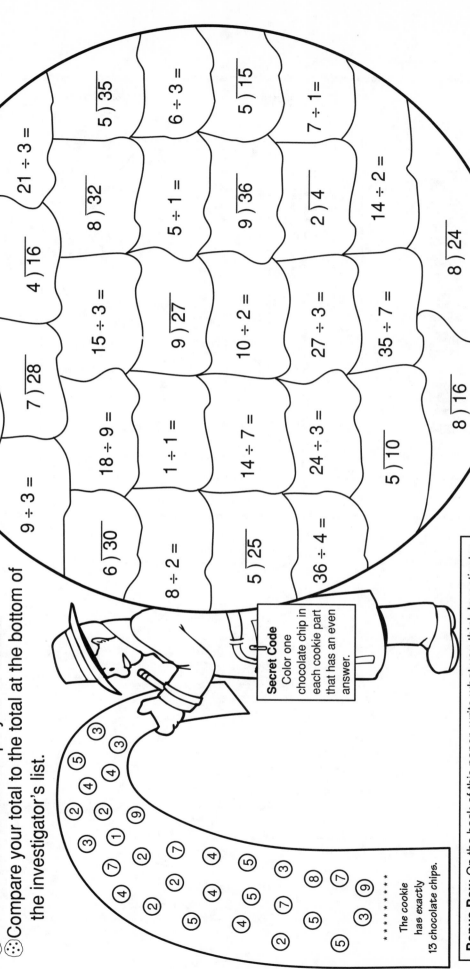

$21 \div 3 =$

$5\overline{)35}$

$6 \div 3 =$

$5\overline{)15}$

$7 \div 1 =$

$5\overline{)20}$

$8\overline{)32}$

$5 \div 1 =$

$9\overline{)36}$

$2\overline{)4}$

$14 \div 2 =$

$12 \div 4 =$

$4\overline{)16}$

$15 \div 3 =$

$9\overline{)27}$

$10 \div 2 =$

$27 \div 3 =$

$35 \div 7 =$

$8\overline{)24}$

$9 \div 3 =$

$7\overline{)28}$

$18 \div 9 =$

$1 \div 1 =$

$14 \div 7 =$

$24 \div 3 =$

$5\overline{)10}$

$8\overline{)16}$

$6\overline{)30}$

$8 \div 2 =$

$5\overline{)25}$

$36 \div 4 =$

Secret Code
Color one chocolate chip in each cookie part that has an even answer.

* * * * * * * * *
The cookie has exactly 13 chocolate chips.

Bonus Box: On the back of this paper, write what you think Investigator Crumb will do now that he's found the missing cookie.

123

Award

Duplicate and present this award to your students to acknowledge their success with division.

Look Who's Sweet On Division!

_____ is one

smart cookie!

Teacher _____

Date _____

©The Education Center, Inc. • *The Best of Teacher's Helper® Math* • TEC3212

Answer Key

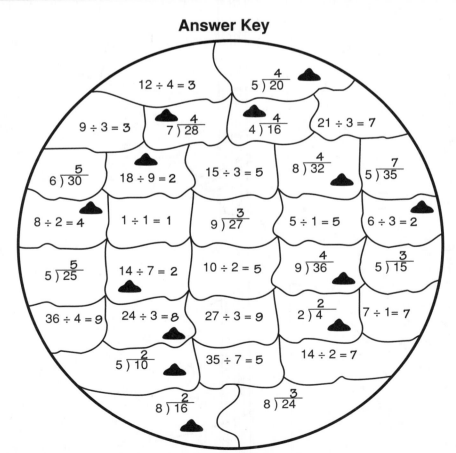

$12 \div 4 = 3$

$5\overline{)20}$ → 4

$9 \div 3 = 3$

$7\overline{)28}$ → 4

$4\overline{)16}$ → 4

$21 \div 3 = 7$

$6\overline{)30}$ → 5

$18 \div 9 = 2$

$15 \div 3 = 5$

$8\overline{)32}$ → 4

$5\overline{)35}$ → 7

$8 \div 2 = 4$

$1 \div 1 = 1$

$9\overline{)27}$ → 3

$5 \div 1 = 5$

$6 \div 3 = 2$

$5\overline{)25}$ → 5

$14 \div 7 = 2$

$10 \div 2 = 5$

$9\overline{)36}$ → 4

$5\overline{)15}$ → 3

$36 \div 4 = 9$

$24 \div 3 = 8$

$27 \div 3 = 9$

$2\overline{)4}$ → 2

$7 \div 1 = 7$

$5\overline{)10}$ → 2

$35 \div 7 = 5$

$14 \div 2 = 7$

$8\overline{)16}$ → 2

$8\overline{)24}$ → 3

Name _____

What's The Chance?

1. LOOK inside your paper bag.
   WRITE the color of each marble on a line.
   In each circle PREDICT how many times you
   will grab each color of marble if you reach
   inside the bag 20 times.

   _____   _____

2. WRITE the marble colors on the lines.
   REACH inside the bag 20 times and GRAB one marble each time.
   For each marble you grab, COLOR one box.

   _____

   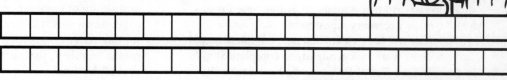

   _____

3. COUNT and RECORD the data you collected
   in the box at the right.

_____	_____
marble color	number
_____	_____
marble color	number

4. COMPARE your data with a classmate's data.
   DESCRIBE what you discover.

   _____

   _____

5. THINK about what you have learned.
   PREDICT what will happen if you repeat
   the activity using two different marbles.

   _____

   _____

   EXPLAIN your prediction.

   _____

   _____

Bonus Box: Trade marbles with a classmate and test your prediction. On the back of this paper, describe the results of your test. Then write a sentence that tells one more thing you have learned about probability.

How To Use This Probability Unit
Pages 125–130

Use this creative collection of reproducibles to investigate probability. It's highly probable that your students will learn plenty and have fun too!

Materials Needed For Each Student

— copy of page 125
— brown paper lunch sack containing two different-colored marbles (For easy use, cut away the top four inches of the sack.)
— crayons
— pencil

How To Use Page 125

1. Have each student complete Step 1. Invite interested students to tell the class what they predict will happen and why.
2. Next have each student complete Steps 2 and 3.
3. Ask each student to add his recorded data together from Step 3 to confirm that it totals 20. Allow time for students to make necessary adjustments.
4. Pair students and have each youngster complete Step 4.
5. Have students work independently to complete Step 5.
6. To complete the Bonus Box activity, have each child trade his sack of marbles with his partner from Step 4.

Background For The Teacher
Probability

When it is stated that one event is more *probable* than another, it means that the event is more likely to happen. Mathematically speaking, a probability is a ratio that tells how likely it is that an event will occur. The probability that a flipped coin will land on heads is 1:2—one chance in two that it will occur. The probability that a tossed die will reveal the numeral 4 is 1:6—one chance in six that a 4 will be rolled.

Students and adults encounter probability in a variety of ways. When a student plays a game that utilizes dice or a spinner, probability is involved. Weather predictions and economic forecasts involve various aspects of probability. When investigating probability, it is important to understand that there are uncertainties and limitations involved when drawing conclusions from the data that is collected.

Information For The Teacher
Page 125

During "What's The Chance?" a student investigates the probability of grabbing one of two colors of marbles from a paper lunch sack. Only two possible outcomes are considered for this activity—grabbing one marble or the other. This means, in theory, that each marble should be grabbed 50 percent of the time.

It is doubtful that the results your youngsters gather will support theoretical probability. This is because the students are recording a small amount of data. The Law of Large Numbers maintains that a small number of trials (like grabbing a marble from a bag or flipping a coin) will yield a wide range of results, which may or may not be close to the expected probability. On the other hand, a large number of trials will give results that are quite close to the expected probability. For example, if a person reaches into a bag that holds two different-colored marbles and grabs one marble for each of 20 tries, it is highly unlikely that she will grab each color of marble ten times. However if a person reaches into the same bag 100 times, it is quite likely that she will grab each color of marble about 50 times.

When a student completes the Bonus Box on page 125, the data she yields may be different from the data she collected in Step 3. Since the number of trials has remained constant, the difference in the data is an example of the Law of Large Numbers (described above) at work.

Answer Key

Answers will vary. See "Information For The Teacher" on this page for clarity.

Name _____

Heads Or Tails?

1. PREDICT how many heads and tails you will get if you flip a coin 20 times.

Heads _____   Tails _____

2. FLIP a coin 20 times.
   For each coin flip, COLOR one box.

Heads

Tails

3. COUNT and RECORD the data you collected.

Heads _____   Tails _____

4. COMPARE your data with a classmate's data.
   DESCRIBE what you discover.

_____

_____

_____

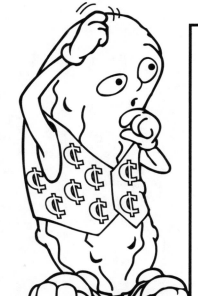

5. THINK about what you have learned.
   PREDICT how many heads and tails you will get if you flip the coin 40 times.

Heads _____   Tails _____

EXPLAIN why you made this prediction.

_____

_____

Bonus Box: Test your prediction. On the back of this paper, describe the results of your test. Then write a sentence that tells one more thing you have learned about probability.

Materials Needed For Each Student

— copy of page 127
— coin
— crayons
— pencil

How To Use Page 127

1. Have each student complete Step 1. Invite interested students to tell the class what they predict will happen and why.
2. Next have each student complete Steps 2 and 3.
3. Ask each student to add his recorded data together from Step 3 to confirm that it totals 20. Allow time for students to make necessary adjustments.
4. Pair students and have each youngster complete Step 4.
5. Have students work independently to complete Step 5 and the Bonus Box activity.

Information For The Teacher
Page 127

During "Heads Or Tails?" a student investigates the probability of flipping a coin and having it land on heads or on tails. Only two possible outcomes are considered when flipping a coin—that it will land on heads or it will land on tails. There is the slimmest chance that the coin could land squarely on its edge; however, this possibility is so highly unlikely that it is not even considered. This means, in theory, that a coin should land on heads 50 percent of the time and on tails 50 percent of the time.

It is doubtful that the results your youngsters gather will support theoretical probability. This is because the students are recording a small number of flips. The Law of Large Numbers maintains that a small number of trials (like coin flips or dice tosses) will yield a wide range of results, which may or may not be close to the expected probability. On the other hand, a large number of trials will give results that are quite close to the expected probability. For example, if a person flips a coin ten times, it is highly unlikely that it will land on heads five times and on tails five times. However, if a person flips a coin 100 times, it is quite likely that it will land on heads about 50 times and on tails about 50 times.

Answer Key

Answers will vary. The data gathered from the Bonus Box activity may more closely resemble theoretical probability (a flipped coin will land on heads 50 percent of the time and on tails 50 percent of the time) because the coin is being flipped more times. See "Information For The Teacher" on this page for clarity.

On A Roll!

1. PREDICT which number will appear the most often when you roll a die.
   CIRCLE your prediction in the box.

1	2	3	4	5	6

2. ROLL the die 24 times.
   For each roll, COLOR one box on the graph.

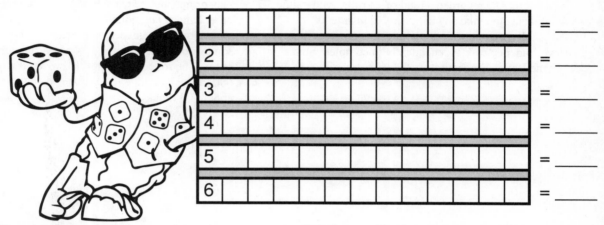

	= _____
1	= _____
2	= _____
3	= _____
4	= _____
5	= _____
6	= _____

3. COUNT and RECORD the data you collected to the right of the graph.

4. COMPARE your data with a classmate's data.
   DESCRIBE what you discover.

   _____

   _____

5. THINK about what you have learned.
   PREDICT how many times you will roll a 6 if you
       roll the die 24 more times.
   WRITE your prediction in the box the pickle is
       holding.

   EXPLAIN why you made this prediction.

   _____

   _____

   _____

Bonus Box:
Stretch your brain!
What if there were
no element of
chance involved in
rolling a die? How
many 6s might you
roll in 30 tries?

Materials Needed For Each Student

— copy of page 129
— die
— crayons
— pencil

How To Use Page 129

1. Have each student complete Step 1. Invite interested students to tell the class what they predict will happen and why.
2. Next have each student complete Steps 2 and 3.
3. Ask each child to add his column of recorded data to confirm that he recorded a total of 24 rolls. Allow time for students to make any necessary adjustments.
4. Pair students and have each youngster complete Step 4.
5. Have students work independently to complete Step 5 and the Bonus Box activity.

Information For The Teacher
Page 129

During "On A Roll!" a student investigates the probability of rolling the numbers 1 through 6. In theory, if an evenly weighted die is used, each of the six numbers has an equal chance of being rolled on any one toss. This would result in each number being rolled one-sixth of the time.

It is doubtful that the results your youngsters gather will support theoretical probability. This is because the students are recording a small number of tosses. The Law of Large Numbers maintains that a small number of trials (like dice tosses or coin flips) will yield a wide range of results, which may or may not be close to the expected probability. On the other hand, a large number of trials will give results that are quite close to the expected probability. For example, if a person tosses a die 12 times, it is not very likely that each number will be rolled two times. However, if a person tosses a die 600 times, it is quite likely that each number will be rolled about 100 times.

Answer Key

Answers will vary. See "Information For The Teacher" on this page for clarity.

Bonus Box Answer: If there were *no* element of chance involved in rolling a die, a person could roll a 6 as many times as he or she wanted! (If the element of chance were perfectly predictable, a person would roll one 6 in every six rolls. This would mean that in 30 rolls a person would roll a 6 five times.)

Pizza By The Slice

Solve the problems.
Draw toppings on the pizza slice.
Use the code.

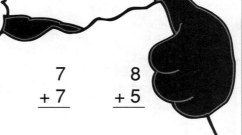

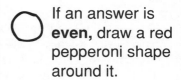

Topping Code

If an answer is **odd,** draw a brown mushroom shape around it.

If an answer is **even,** draw a red pepperoni shape around it.

$$\begin{array}{r} 7 \\ +7 \end{array} \qquad \begin{array}{r} 8 \\ +5 \end{array}$$

$$\begin{array}{r} 14 \\ -6 \end{array} \qquad \begin{array}{r} 12 \\ -8 \end{array} \qquad \begin{array}{r} 5 \\ +6 \end{array}$$

$$\begin{array}{r} 9 \\ +4 \end{array} \quad \begin{array}{r} 12 \\ -9 \end{array} \quad \begin{array}{r} 4 \\ +3 \end{array} \quad \begin{array}{r} 6 \\ +6 \end{array} \quad \begin{array}{r} 7 \\ +9 \end{array}$$

$16 - 8 = $ _____ $9 - 3 = $ _____

$13 - 4 = $ _____ $8 + 7 = $ _____

$$\begin{array}{r} 9 \\ +8 \end{array} \; \begin{array}{r} 13 \\ -5 \end{array} \; \begin{array}{r} 3 \\ +6 \end{array} \; \begin{array}{r} 6 \\ +4 \end{array} \; \begin{array}{r} 18 \\ -9 \end{array} \; \begin{array}{r} 10 \\ -5 \end{array} \; \begin{array}{r} 11 \\ -4 \end{array}$$

$6 + 7 = $ _____ $3 + 7 = $ _____ $9 + 2 = $ _____ $14 - 8 = $ _____

$8 - 4 = $ _____ $15 - 7 = $ _____ $5 + 7 = $ _____

Bonus Box: On the back of this sheet, draw and color
a slice of your favorite kind of pizza.

How To Use This Thematic Math Unit
Pages 131–140

These pizza-related math reproducibles feature five scrumptious math skills—one per student page. Whether you use the activities to reinforce math skills or to better determine each child's math capabilities, the results are sure to be tasty! You'll also find a delicious assortment of pizza-related books, a hot-'n'-spicy song, a kid-pleasing recipe, and directions for an easy-to-make center. Any way you slice it, this unit adds up to lots of fun!

Extension Activities

— Integrate music into your pizza math practice by singing this song to the tune of "Oh, I Wish I Were An Oscar Mayer® Weiner." Sing the song as a round, or choose a different child to provide the pizza of choice (for example, "a pepperoni pizza" or "an extra cheesy pizza") for each of several verses.

> Oh, I wish I were [a hot and spicy pizza].
> That is what I'd truly like to be.
> For if I were [a hot and spicy pizza],
> Everyone would be in love with me!

— Create this appetizing math center in a jiffy! Decorate three, eight-inch poster-board circles to resemble pizzas. Cut each pizza into several different-sized slices; then label the slices of each pizza with different math problems that share a common answer. Laminate the cutouts for durability. Store the pizza slices in a resealable plastic bag. Place the bag, a supply of scrap paper, and three aluminum pizza pans at a center. A student solves each problem on scrap paper, then sorts the pizza slices by placing the slices with like answers on the same pizza pan. To check her work, she arranges the slices on each pan to form a pizza.

Book Corner
Pizza

Pizza! • Written by Teresa Martino & Illustrated by Brigid Faranda • Steck-Vaughn Company, 1998

A Job For Wittilda • Written by Caralyn Buehner & Illustrated by Mark Buehner • Dial Books For Young Readers, 1993

Little Nino's Pizzeria • Written & Illustrated by Karen Barbour • Harcourt Brace Jovanovich, Publishers; 1990

Extra Cheese, Please!: Mozzarella's Journey From Cow To Pizza • Written by Cris Peterson & Photographed by Alvis Upitis • Boyds Mills Press, Inc.; 1994

Answer Key

Name_____

Which Topping Is Tops?

Graph the pizza toppings that were ordered. Use the information in the boxes.

Panda's Pizzeria

pepperoni	8
mushrooms	5
pineapple	1
onions	2
ham	2
sausage	6

ham	5
onions	1
pepperoni	4
mushrooms	4
pineapple	5
sausage	5

Pizza Toppings

(bar graph, y-axis 0–12, x-axis: pineapple, mushrooms, pepperoni, ham, onions, sausage)

Use the graph to answer the questions.

1. Which topping was ordered the most?_____

2. Which topping was ordered the least?_____

3. How many times was sausage ordered?_____

4. How many more times was ham ordered than pineapple?_____

5. How many more times were mushrooms ordered than onions?_____

6. Which three toppings were ordered the most?_____

_____

Bonus Box: If every mushroom pizza also had pepperoni, how many pepperoni pizzas did not have mushrooms? _____

Answer Key

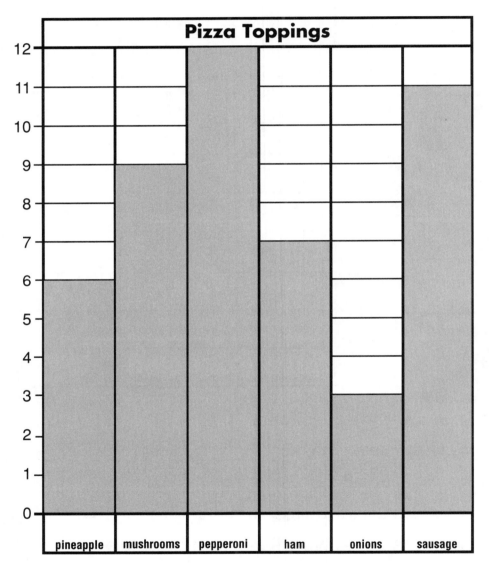

1. pepperoni
2. onions
3. 11 times
4. one more time
5. six more times
6. pepperoni, sausage, mushrooms

Bonus Box Answer: three pepperoni pizzas

Lots Of Leftovers

Cut out each pizza.
Decide how much of the pizza is left.
Glue the pizza on its matching pan.

$\frac{1}{3}$

$\frac{1}{4}$

$\frac{2}{3}$

$\frac{3}{8}$

$\frac{1}{5}$

$\frac{2}{6}$

$\frac{1}{2}$

$\frac{4}{6}$

$\frac{1}{8}$

$\frac{3}{4}$

$\frac{2}{5}$

$\frac{4}{4}$

Bonus Box: Peppy Panda had the least amount of pizza left on her pizza pan. Use a yellow crayon to circle Peppy's pizza pan.

©The Education Center, Inc. • *The Best of* Teacher's Helper® *Math* • TEC3212

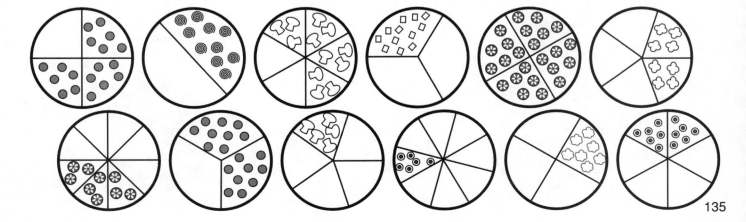

Answer Key

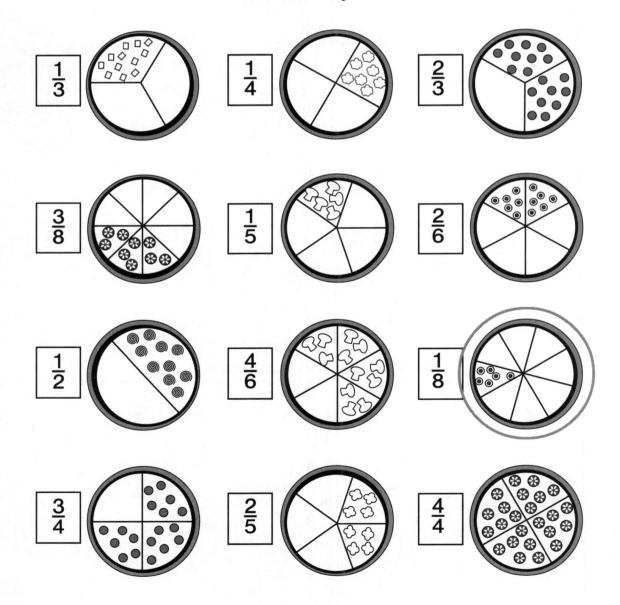

Name _____

Pizza Makings

Count the money in each row.
Write the amount on the pizza pan.
Color the ingredient you can buy
   with that amount of money.

Panda's Pineapple 31¢

Perfect Pizza Crust Mix 78¢

Tasty Ham 92¢

Yummy Pizza Sauce 47¢

O-Look Olives 58¢

Fresh Mushrooms 63¢

Green Pepper 24¢

Hot 'n' Spicy Pepperoni 99¢

The Best Cheese 80¢

A. ___¢

B. ___¢

C. ___¢

D. ___¢

E. ___¢

F. ___¢

G. ___¢

H. ___¢

Bonus Box: Find the ingredient that you did not color. On the back of this page, write the price of that ingredient. Draw and color five coins that equal the amount.

Follow-Up Activity

These easy-to-bake individual pizzas make a delicious follow-up activity to "Pizza Makings" on page 137. If desired, duplicate student copies of the recipe below for students to carry home.

Miniature Pizzas

Ingredients:
refrigerated biscuit dough (one biscuit per pizza)
prepared pizza sauce
mozzarella cheese, grated
a variety of pizza toppings (pepperoni, mushrooms, green peppers, pineapple, etc.)

Supplies:
ungreased baking sheet(s)
spoon(s)
spatula
waxed paper
oven

Directions:
Preheat oven to 425°F. To make a miniature pizza, place the dough of one biscuit on waxed paper. Use your hands to flatten and shape the dough; then use a spoon to spread pizza sauce all over the dough except for the edges. Cover the sauce with a layer of grated cheese and place desired pizza toppings on top of the cheese. Peel away the waxed paper from the bottom of the pizza and place the pizza on an ungreased baking sheet. Bake for approximately 10 minutes, until the cheese is melted and the crust is golden brown. Use the spatula to carefully remove the pizza from the baking sheet.

Answer Key
A. 47¢
B. 63¢
C. 99¢
D. 58¢
E. 80¢
F. 92¢
G. 31¢
H. 24¢

Bonus Box Answer: 78¢: 1 half-dollar, 1 quarter, 3 pennies

Name _____

Speedy Delivery

Write the time on the lines below each clock.
Find the matching time below. Color the box red.

____ : ____   ____ : ____   ____ : ____   ____ : ____   ____ : ____

____ : ____   ____ : ____   ____ : ____   ____ : ____   ____ : ____

____ : ____   ____ : ____   ____ : ____   ____ : ____   ____ : ____

7:45	12:00	4:15	5:45	8:30
3:30				10:15
				3:45
9:00				6:30
1:15	6:00	9:45	11:30	2:00

Panda's Pizzeria

Bear In Mind—We Deliver On Time!

Panda's Pizzeria

Answer Key

3:30	4:15	6:00	11:30	5:45
9:00	6:30	10:15	2:00	3:45
7:45	12:00	8:30	9:45	1:15

Name _____

Pots Of Gold

Write two <u>true</u> number sentences on each pot.
Use the three numbers on the coins.
You must use one number twice.

> means greater than

< means less than

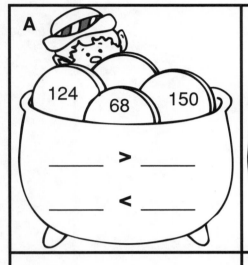

A

124 68 150

_____ **>** _____

_____ **<** _____

B

999 509 95

_____ **>** _____

_____ **<** _____

C

73 703 337

_____ **>** _____

_____ **<** _____

D

612 621 206

_____ **>** _____

_____ **<** _____

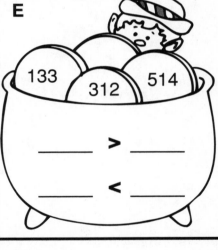

E

133 312 514

_____ **>** _____

_____ **<** _____

F

448 840 484

_____ **>** _____

_____ **<** _____

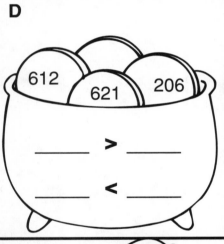

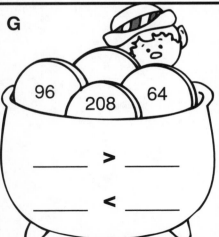

G

96 208 64

_____ **>** _____

_____ **<** _____

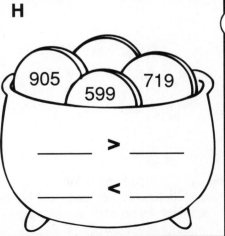

H

905 599 719

_____ **>** _____

_____ **<** _____

The sum of the coins is greater than 350.

There is a leprechaun guarding the pot!

The coin values are all even.

Bonus Box: Can you find the lucky pot of gold? Use the leprechaun's clues. Color the coins in the lucky pot.

How To Use This Thematic Math Unit
Pages 141–148

A treasure of math reviews awaits your youngsters! Plan to incorporate the reproducible activities into your math studies during the month of March.

Rainbow Rounding

Name _____

Follow these steps to round each rainbow number to the nearest ten:
1. On the first cloud write the ten that comes before the rainbow number.
2. On the second cloud write the ten that comes after the rainbow number.
3. Round the rainbow number.
4. Circle your answer.
The first one is done for you!

If there are five or more ones, round up!

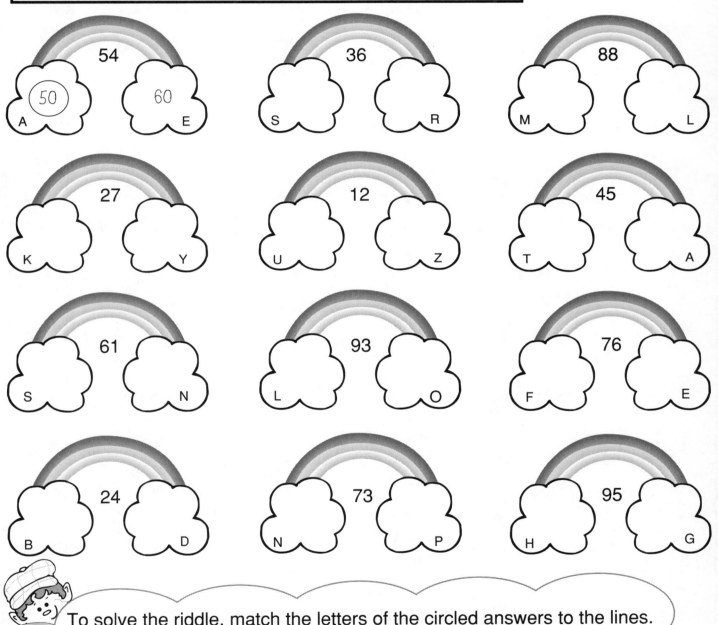

54   (50) A   60 E

36   S   R

88   M   L

27   K   Y

12   U   Z

45   T   A

61   S   N

93   L   O

76   F   E

24   B   D

73   N   P

95   H   G

To solve the riddle, match the letters of the circled answers to the lines.

What is a leprechaun's favorite kind of hamburger?

<u>A</u>   ___   ___   <u>A</u>   ___   ___   ___   ___   ___   ___   ___   ___   ___   ___
50   20   90   50   40   70   80   30   20   10   40   100   80   40

Answer Key

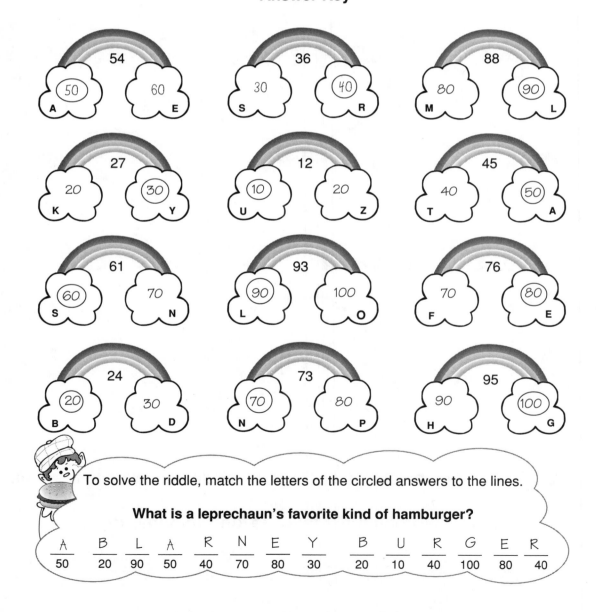

54
A (50) E 60

36
S 30 R (40)

88
M 80 L (90)

27
K 20 Y (30)

12
U (10) Z 20

45
T 40 A (50)

61
S (60) N 70

93
L (90) O 100

76
F 70 E (80)

24
B (20) D 30

73
N (70) P 80

95
H 90 G (100)

To solve the riddle, match the letters of the circled answers to the lines.

What is a leprechaun's favorite kind of hamburger?

A	B	L	A	R	N	E	Y	B	U	R	G	E	R
50	20	90	50	40	70	80	30	20	10	40	100	80	40

Name _____

Shapes And A Shenanigan!

How well do you know your solid shapes?
Color and cut out each picture below.
Match and glue each picture to a shape shelf.

What's a shenanigan?
It's a trick!
Look for one shape
that cannot be shelved.

McCool's
Ice-Cream
Holders

Fragile! Crushable cones inside!

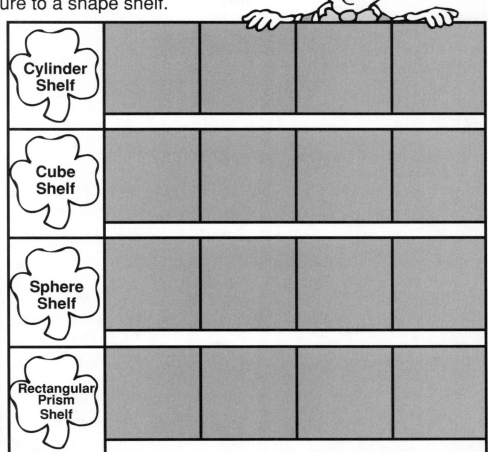

Cylinder Shelf

Cube Shelf

Sphere Shelf

Rectangular Prism Shelf

Answer the questions.

1. How many cylinders? _____

2. How many rectangular prisms? _____

3. How many more spheres than cubes? _____

4. Which picture could not be shelved? _____

Bonus Box: Glue the picture that could not be shelved on the back of this paper. Write the name of the shape beside the picture. If you are stumped, look for a clue on this side of your paper.

How To Use Page 145

Before introducing the activity, review solid shapes with your students. If desired, display samples of the solid shapes featured on the page (cylinder, cube, sphere, and rectangular prism) and ask students to identify each one. Or have students locate examples of each of the four shapes in the classroom.

Answer Key
(Order of answers on each shelf will vary.)

Cylinder Shelf: Shamrock Soup, O'Kitty's Fancy Food, McCrisp's Crunchy Potatoes, St. Pat's Paper Towels
Cube Shelf: McSneezy's Soft Tissues, Wee Bits Of Sugar
Sphere Shelf: McBubble Gum, Irish Orange, Green Cheese
Rectangular Prism Shelf: Leprechaun's Lasagna, Irish Crackers, Lucky Puffs, Blarney Butter

1. four cylinders
2. four rectangular prisms
3. one more
4. McCool's Ice-Cream Holders

Bonus Box Answer: cone

Name _____

Strike It Rich!

Solve the problems.

♣♣♣ Lucky Gameboard ♣♣♣			

©The Education Center, Inc. • *The Best of* Teacher's Helper® *Math* • TEC3212

♣ 384 + 215	♣ 197 − 182	♣ 450 + 138	♣ 974 − 553	♣ 263 − 151
♣ 627 + 242	♣ 764 − 432	♣ 622 + 357	♣ 503 + 494	♣ 858 − 425
♣ 241 + 624	♣ 578 − 363	♣ 734 + 154	♣ 693 − 472	♣ 698 − 346

Materials Needed For Each Student
— construction-paper copy of page 147
— pencil
— scissors
— glue
— crayons
— 15 one-inch squares of gold construction paper to use as markers
— optional: one resealable plastic bag for storage of game markers

How To Use Page 147
1. Distribute the first two materials listed above.
2. As students complete the activity on page 147, use the answer key to complete an extra copy of the problems on page 147. Cut on the dotted lines and store the resulting cutouts in a container.
3. When all students have finished, check the activity as a class and have students make necessary corrections.
4. Distribute the rest of the materials listed above.
5. Have each student decorate a free space on his blank gameboard.
6. Then instruct each child to cut on the dotted lines and randomly glue one cutout to each blank gameboard space.
7. Announce the type of game to be played, such as four in a row or four corners. Instruct students to declare "Gold!" if they are winners.
8. One at a time, draw a cutout from the container and read aloud the problem and its answer. Each student then places a game marker on the corresponding square on his gameboard.
9. If desired, have the winner of the first game become the caller of the second game, and so on.
10. At the conclusion of the activity, collect the game markers in a resealable plastic bag and store them for future use. If desired, give each participant a gold nugget—a piece of candy that's wrapped in gold foil!

How To Reuse Or Reprogram The Gameboard
1. White-out the problems on a copy of page 147; then make several copies of the page.
2. To create a new game, program an altered copy of the page (from Step 1) with 15 desired math problems.
3. Duplicate the new gameboard and create a corresponding answer key.
4. Follow the instructions under "How To Use Page 147."

Answer Key

384 + 215 599	197 − 182 15	450 + 138 588	974 − 553 421	263 − 151 112
627 + 242 869	764 − 432 332	622 + 357 979	503 + 494 997	858 − 425 433
241 + 624 865	578 − 363 215	734 + 154 888	693 − 472 221	698 − 346 352

Davy's Far-Fetched Tales

Davy Crockett liked to tell tall tales about himself!
Read each sentence. Look at the number choices.
In each blank write the number Davy might have used.

1. I was such a big baby I slept in a _____-pound turtle shell.
   600   **6**   **60**

2. When I was only _____ years old, I weighed 200 pounds.
   25   **16**   **8**

3. As a boy I drank _____ gallons of buffalo milk a day.
   2   **20**   **5**

4. I'm such a good shot I can hit a fly _____ feet away.
   50   **5**   **500**

5. I can cut down any tree with _____ swings of my axe!
   10   **50**   **2**

6. One time I captured 105 bears in _____ months!
   15   **7**   **23**

7. I wrestled a boa constrictor for _____ days without stopping.
   2   **10**   **7**

8. When I met Sally Ann Thunder Ann Whirlwind, my heart beat 500 times in _____ minutes.
   10   **2**   **5**

9. When Sally agreed to marry me, I jumped _____ feet off the ground!
   2   **10**   **15**

10. Sally and I agreed to have at least _____ children.
    13   **30**   **3**

Bonus Box: On the back of this paper, write three *true* sentences about yourself.
Use a different number in each sentence. Choose from the numbers below.

     3   5   10   20   50   100

How To Use This Tall-Tale Math Unit
Pages 149–160

Incorporate these math activities into a study of tall tales, or use them as desired to reinforce the featured skills. Whatever you choose, math practice is sure to have *enormous* appeal!

How To Use Page 149

Emphasize that Davy Crockett liked to tell far-fetched tales about himself—the more far-fetched, the better. To complete the activity, challenge students to choose numbers that create the *tallest* tales. Caution students to read carefully. If desired, divulge to students that sometimes a lesser number creates a taller tale than a greater number!

Book Corner
Davy Crockett

Sally Ann Thunder Ann Whirlwind Crockett • Retold & Illustrated by Steven Kellogg • William Morrow and Company, Inc.; 1995

Davy Crockett, Young Pioneer • Written by Laurence Santrey & Illustrated by Francis Livingston • Troll Associates, Inc.; 1989

Background For The Teacher
Tall Tales

Tall tales existed long before the first pioneers came to America, but it was on the American frontier where tall tales found their footing. Telling stories was a way for Americans to come to terms with the challenges of daily life. When the work was done, they'd gather around the fire and tell tales. These rugged folks weren't interested in telling tales the same way they'd heard them, so the stories got bigger and better with each telling. A spirit of good-natured one-upmanship often resulted, which led to bouts of boasting, outrageous exaggeration, and outlandish tales!

Tall-tale characters were born from various combinations of historical facts, the storytelling of ordinary people, and the imaginations of professional writers. Johnny Appleseed and Davy Crockett were real people who lived during the early 1800s. Pecos Bill and Slue-Foot Sue are fictitious characters. Although no one person could ever do the kinds of things attributed to these larger-than-life characters, their spirit and determination to succeed are 100-percent believable!

Davy Crockett: 1786–1836

The real Davy Crockett—who became one of the most famous frontiersmen in the history of the United States—was born in Greene County, Tennessee, on August 17, 1786. He was a first-rate hunter and soldier who used his reputation to build a successful political career. Crockett was well known for telling tall tales about himself and for his political pranks. Crockett died at the Alamo in 1836, fighting for Texas in its struggle for independence from Mexico. Following his death, a series of small books that contained exaggerated tales about Crockett's early life were published. These far-fetched tales helped create the legendary character of Davy Crockett.

Answer Key
1. 600
2. 8
3. 20
4. 500
5. 2
6. 7
7. 10
8. 2
9. 15
10. 30

Tall-Tale Math
Addition and subtraction:
2-digit without regrouping

Pecos Bill's Lasso

Snakes alive! Look at the problems Pecos Bill has rounded up!
Solve each problem.
Color the matching answer on Pecos Bill's rattlesnake lasso.

$$57 + 11$$ $$47 - 24$$ $$98 - 43$$ $$25 + 22$$

$$36 - 12$$ $$61 + 28$$ $$83 + 15$$ $$93 - 62$$

$$33 + 12$$ $$82 - 61$$ $$67 - 35$$ $$44 + 32$$

$$75 + 24$$ $$78 - 25$$ $$39 + 40$$

$$65 - 13$$ $$14 + 55$$ $$59 - 22$$

$$84 - 40$$ $$26 + 51$$ $$76 - 14$$

Lasso numbers: 32, 98, 89, 68, 55, 21, 88, 53, 77, 45, 99, 37, 69, 79, 76, 31, 47, 23, 44, 62, 24, 52

Bonus Box: Find the answer you did not color. On the back of this paper, write an addition problem and a subtraction problem that both equal this answer. Then color the answer on the snake. You may color the rest of the rattler and Pecos Bill too! Yahoo!

Background For The Teacher
Pecos Bill

Who is the roughest, toughest, meanest cowboy hero in American folklore? Without a doubt, it's Pecos Bill! According to legend, Pecos Bill was born in eastern Texas during the 1830s. He is the legendary inventor of roping, branding, and other cowboy skills. He is also credited with inventing the six-shooter and train robbery. Later in life he fell head over heels in love and married Slue-Foot Sue—a legendary heroine with Texas roots.

The legend of Pecos Bill began with a magazine article written in 1923 by an American journalist named Edward O'Reilly. O'Reilly patterned Pecos Bill after Paul Bunyan, Davy Crockett, and other legendary frontier heroes. O'Reilly's original tale perpetuated many more far-fetched tales about the wild and reckless cowpoke named Pecos Bill.

Book Corner
Pecos Bill

Pecos Bill: The Roughest, Toughest, Best • Written by Patsy Jensen & Illustrated by Ben Mahan • Troll Associates, Inc.; 1995

Pecos Bill • Retold & Illustrated by Steven Kellogg • Mulberry Books, 1992

Answer Key

57 + 11 **68**	47 − 24 **23**	98 − 43 **55**	25 + 22 **47**
36 − 12 **24**	61 + 28 **89**	83 + 15 **98**	93 − 62 **31**
33 + 12 **45**	82 − 61 **21**	67 − 35 **32**	44 + 32 **76**
75 + 24 **99**	78 − 25 **53**	39 + 40 **79**	
65 − 13 **52**	14 + 55 **69**	59 − 22 **37**	
84 − 40 **44**	26 + 51 **77**	76 − 14 **62**	

Bonus Box Answer: The unused answer is 88.

Name_____

Paul's Pancake House

Menu

Silver Dollar Flapjacks	$5.45
Bunyan's Buttermilk Pancakes	$2.19
Babe's Blueberry Pancakes	$3.27
Hefty Hotcakes	$3.53
Chocolate Chip Pancakes	$4.08
Fresh Milk	$1.22
Orange Juice	$1.49
Extra Syrup (one gallon)	$2.35
Extra Butter	$1.09

Paul Bunyan has many orders to fill!
While Paul is cooking, find the totals of the orders shown.
Show your work in your order booklet.

Order 1:   Chocolate Chip Pancakes, Fresh Milk

Order 2:   Silver Dollar Flapjacks, Extra Syrup

Order 3:   Bunyan's Buttermilk Pancakes, Extra Butter

Order 4:   Babe's Blueberry Pancakes, Orange Juice

Order 5:   Hefty Hotcakes, Orange Juice

Order 6:   Chocolate Chip Pancakes, Extra Butter

Order 7:   Silver Dollar Flapjacks, Babe's Blueberry Pancakes

Order 8:   Bunyan's Buttermilk Pancakes, Fresh Milk

Order 9:   Hefty Hotcakes, Extra Butter, Fresh Milk

Order 10:   _____

_____

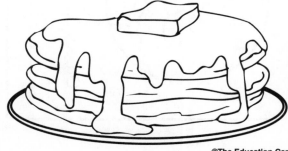

What would you order at Paul's Pancake House?
Write your order on the lines above.
Find the total of your order.
Show your work in your order booklet.

Materials Needed For Each Student

— copy of page 153
— construction-paper copy of the booklet cover below
— ten 2 1/4" x 3 1/2" blank booklet pages
— scissors
— crayons or markers
— pencil
— access to a stapler

Directions For Each Student

1. Personalize, color, and cut out the booklet cover.
2. Fold the cover in half along the thin line.
3. Stack and staple the booklet pages inside the booklet cover.
4. Number the booklet pages from one to ten.
5. Complete page 153. Calculate the total of each order on the corresponding booklet page.

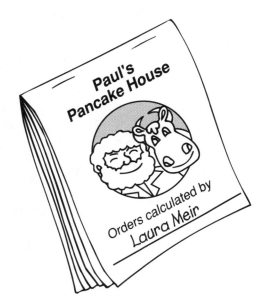

Background For The Teacher
Paul Bunyan

Paul Bunyan—a giant lumberjack in American folklore—became famous for his great strength and incredible logging feats. According to legend, Paul invented logging in the Pacific Northwest and is responsible for many of America's physical features. For example Paul is credited with clearing all the trees from the Dakotas (to make the land suitable for farming), scooping out the Great Lakes (to provide drinking water for his giant blue ox, Babe), and creating the Grand Canyon (when he accidentally dropped his axe)!

No one knows for sure how the legend of Paul Bunyan began. Some historians think it might have developed from old French folktales about giants that were passed on by French-Canadian lumberjacks. Paul's popular image was fueled by the press, advertising, and books written for children. During the 1920s Paul Bunyan tales were a popular feature in many newspapers. Since then this legendary hero has been featured in ballets, dramas, operas, numerous advertisements, and children's books.

Book Corner
Paul Bunyan

Paul Bunyan And His Blue Ox • Written by Patsy Jensen & Illustrated by Jean Pidgeon • Troll Associates, Inc; 1994

Paul Bunyan • Retold & Illustrated by Steven Kellogg • William Morrow And Company, Inc.; 1985

Answer Key

Order 1:	$ 5.30	**Order 6:**	$ 5.17
Order 2:	$ 7.80	**Order 7:**	$ 8.72
Order 3:	$ 3.28	**Order 8:**	$ 3.41
Order 4:	$ 4.76	**Order 9:**	$ 5.84
Order 5:	$ 5.02	**Order 10:**	Answers will vary.

Booklet Cover

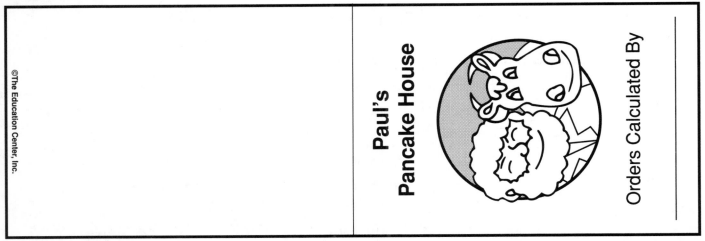

Paul's Pancake House

Orders Calculated By

Name_____

Tall-Tale Math
Subtraction: 3-digit with
regrouping over zeros

Sally Ann's At It Again!

Sally Ann Thunder Ann Whirlwind Crockett has conquered a gang of gators!
See if you can conquer these subtraction problems!

Solve each problem. Show your work.
Cross out the matching answer on an alligator.

$$\begin{array}{r} 406 \\ -218 \\ \hline \end{array}$$ $$\begin{array}{r} 701 \\ -334 \\ \hline \end{array}$$ $$\begin{array}{r} 601 \\ -328 \\ \hline \end{array}$$ $$\begin{array}{r} 304 \\ -145 \\ \hline \end{array}$$

$$\begin{array}{r} 308 \\ -199 \\ \hline \end{array}$$ $$\begin{array}{r} 401 \\ -386 \\ \hline \end{array}$$ $$\begin{array}{r} 102 \\ -74 \\ \hline \end{array}$$ $$\begin{array}{r} 508 \\ -139 \\ \hline \end{array}$$

$$\begin{array}{r} 103 \\ -46 \\ \hline \end{array}$$ $$\begin{array}{r} 907 \\ -89 \\ \hline \end{array}$$ $$\begin{array}{r} 605 \\ -166 \\ \hline \end{array}$$ $$\begin{array}{r} 704 \\ -498 \\ \hline \end{array}$$

$$\begin{array}{r} 807 \\ -569 \\ \hline \end{array}$$ $$\begin{array}{r} 606 \\ -219 \\ \hline \end{array}$$ $$\begin{array}{r} 906 \\ -37 \\ \hline \end{array}$$ $$\begin{array}{r} 405 \\ -328 \\ \hline \end{array}$$

$$\begin{array}{r} 205 \\ -127 \\ \hline \end{array}$$ $$\begin{array}{r} 708 \\ -359 \\ \hline \end{array}$$ $$\begin{array}{r} 803 \\ -497 \\ \hline \end{array}$$ $$\begin{array}{r} 202 \\ -59 \\ \hline \end{array}$$

$$\begin{array}{r} 902 \\ -455 \\ \hline \end{array}$$ $$\begin{array}{r} 504 \\ -277 \\ \hline \end{array}$$ $$\begin{array}{r} 807 \\ -318 \\ \hline \end{array}$$ $$\begin{array}{r} 503 \\ -245 \\ \hline \end{array}$$

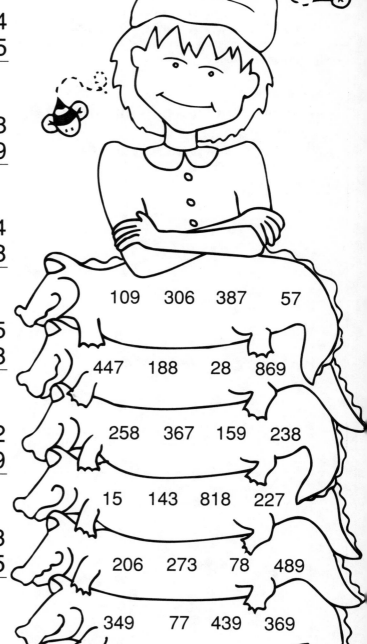

109   306   387   57

447   188   28   869

258   367   159   238

15   143   818   227

206   273   78   489

349   77   439   369

Bonus Box: Sally Ann Thunder Ann Whirlwind Crockett is a one-of-a-
kind lady with a one-of-a-kind name! Write her name on the back of this
paper. Use the letters in her name to spell 20 different words!

Background For The Teacher
Sally Ann Thunder Ann Whirlwind Crockett

You won't find Sally Ann Thunder Ann Whirlwind Crockett in any history book, but that hasn't stopped this gritty gal from becoming an American frontier legend. A reference to Sally Ann—Davy Crockett's fictional wife—appears in the Davy Crockett almanacs that were published from 1834 to 1856. When Sally Ann saved Davy Crockett's life, it was love at first sight for the colossal couple—or so the story goes! In addition to being Davy's wife and an authentic American frontier legend, Sally Ann Thunder Ann Whirlwind Crockett is a tribute to the backwoods women of Tennessee and Kentucky. These rugged frontier women endured the same hardships as the men when they tried to carve out a life on the formidable frontier.

Book Corner
Sally Ann Thunder Ann Whirlwind Crockett

Sally Ann Thunder Ann Whirlwind Crockett • Retold & Illustrated by Steven Kellogg • William Morrow and Company, Inc.; 1995

Answer Key

Row One:	188	367	273	159
Row Two:	109	15	28	369
Row Three:	57	818	439	206
Row Four:	238	387	869	77
Row Five:	78	349	306	143
Row Six:	447	227	489	258

Hammering With John Henry

Hammer out this track of multiplication facts!
In each ○, copy the number on John's hammer.
Multiply.

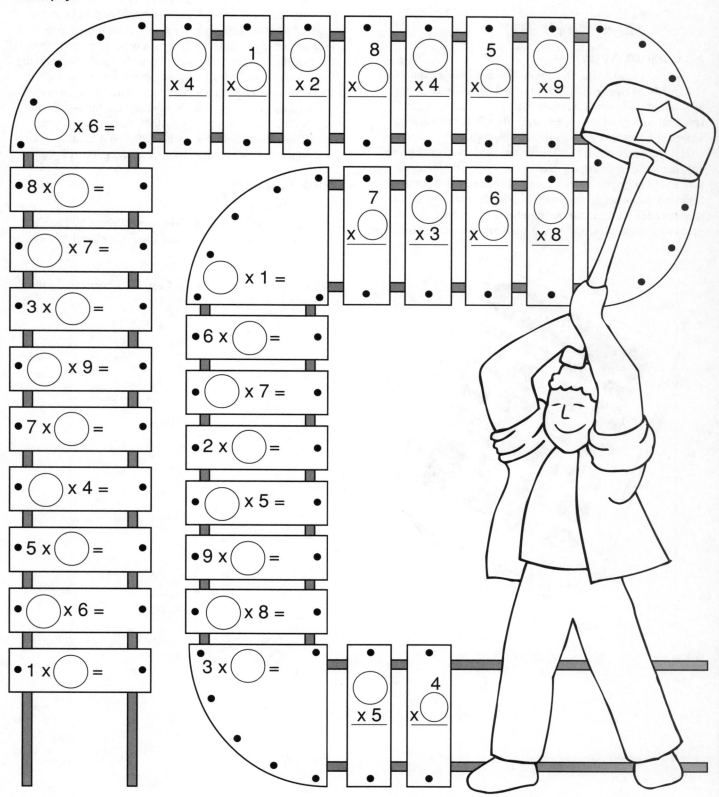

○ x 6 =

○ x 4

1 x ○

○ x 2

8 x ○

○ x 4

5 x ○

○ x 9

7 x ○

○ x 3

6 x ○

○ x 8

8 x ○ =

○ x 7 =

3 x ○ =

○ x 9 =

7 x ○ =

○ x 4 =

5 x ○ =

○ x 6 =

1 x ○ =

○ x 1 =

6 x ○ =

○ x 7 =

2 x ○ =

○ x 5 =

9 x ○ =

○ x 8 =

3 x ○ =

○ x 5

4 x ○

How To Use Page 157

1. Make a copy of page 157. Program the ☆ on John Henry's hammer with a desired factor; then duplicate student copies plus one. (Use the extra copy to make an answer key.)
2. Distribute the student copies and have each child complete the activity as directed.
3. If desired, repeat steps one and two (above) for each of several factors. Every few days have students hammer out a new track with John Henry!

Extension Activity

Ask your students if they think they could beat a machine, just like John Henry did. To find out, stage a student-against-machine race! Distribute student copies of page157 (programmed as in step one above); then have the students write the factor that appears in John Henry's hammer in each circle. Next pair students and give one student in each pair a calculator. On your signal, each student pair completes the activity—one partner uses the calculator and the other uses his mind. Students may be surprised by the outcome of this race between student and machine! If desired, have the partners switch roles, and repeat the activity a second time.

Background For The Teacher
John Henry

Who was the biggest, fastest, strongest steel-driving man who ever lived? That would be John Henry—African-American laborer and folklore hero! Whether there was ever an actual person named John Henry is not certain. What is certain is that in the early 1870s, the Big Bend Tunnel on the Chesapeake And Ohio Railroad was being built in West Virginia. The railroad workers used long-handled hammers to pound steel drills into the rock so that blasting explosives could be put in place. One day a man brought an experimental steam drill to the site and claimed that the machine could dig a hole faster than 20 workers using hammers. Some records indicate that there was an actual man named John Henry who was crushed by falling rock shortly after the race—which the workers won. Through the ballads, songs, and stories written about him, John Henry is a positive reminder of the importance of courage, determination, and goodwill.

Book Corner
John Henry

John Henry And His Mighty Hammer • Written by Patsy Jensen & Illustrated by Roseanne Litzinger • Troll Associates, Inc.; 1994

John Henry • Written by Julius Lester & Illustrated by Jerry Pinkney • Dial Books, 1994